THE
ULTIMATE
TEACHING
MANUAL

A website to accompany this book is available online at:
http://education.dixie.continuumbooks.com
   Please visit the link and register with us to receive your password
and access these downloadable resources.
   If you experience any problems accessing the resources, please
contact Continuum at: info@continuumbooks.com

Also available from Continuum

The Trainee Primary Teacher's Handbook, Janet Bell and Gererd Dixie
The Trainee Secondary Teacher's Handbook, Gererd Dixie
Managing your Classroom, Gererd Dixie

THE
ULTIMATE
TEACHING
MANUAL

A ROUTE TO SUCCESS FOR BEGINNING TEACHERS

Gererd Dixie

continuum

Continuum International Publishing Group

The Tower Building   80 Maiden Lane
11 York Road   Suite 704
London   New York
SE1 7NX   NY 10038

www.continuumbooks.com

The parrot, cowboy, bomb, fisherman, mushroom, toucan and two-can images were kindly provided by Peter Rennoldson.

British Library Cataloguing-in-Publication Data
A catalogue record for this book is available from the British Library.

ISBN: 978-1-4411-8886-1 (paperback)

Library of Congress Cataloging-in-Publication Data
Dixie, Gererd.
The ultimate teaching manual : a route to success for beginning teachers / Gererd Dixie.
      p. cm.
   Includes index.
   ISBN 978-1-4411-8886-1 (alk. paper)
  1. First year teachers--Handbooks, manuals, etc. 2. Teacher orientation--Handbooks, manuals, etc. 3. Teaching--Handbooks, manuals, etc. I. Title.
   LB2844.1.N4D59 2011
   371.1--dc22
                              2010038583

Typeset by Saxon Graphics Ltd, Derby

Contents

Preface

The 'light bulb' moment that first prompted me to think about producing teacher guidance in this format occurred during a highly frustrating car journey on a heavily congested main road that was totally unsuited to such high volumes of traffic.

As I crawled along at about 20 miles an hour, I became increasingly aware of the vast number of information and warning signs littering the roadside. Although these signs have been designed to both inform and warn drivers of the potential hazards ahead, it is interesting to note that this particular road has a reputation for its high accident rate and for being extremely challenging to even the most patient and skilful of drivers. So, if the warning signs are there, why is it that these signs are ignored by so many, and why is it that there are such high casualty figures for this particular road? The tendency for drivers not to act upon the advice and information provided for them set me thinking about the similarities between a journey such as this and the journey involved in a teaching career. Although the warning signs are there for all to see, it is fair to say that behaviour and learning-related problems are abundant in many of our schools today. The fundamental premise of this book is that teaching is a journey – that planning, preparation and forethought are required to presage the making of this journey and that even the most organized and prepared of teachers are likely to come across professional hazards along the way. I use the term 'professional hazards' to describe a number of situations, some of which are:

- where poor pupil behaviour proves to be counteractive to learning;
- where lack of motivation and/or conflict may occur because the learning needs of individual pupils are not being met;
- where teachers become embroiled in conflict with pupils;
- where conflict with colleagues can have a negative effect on pupils' learning;
- where poor working relationships with pupils occur.

The purpose of this manual is to signal and explore the professional hazards likely to be experienced by beginning teachers. I will do this by using the analogies of conventional information, warning and command signs taken from the *Highway Code*. I will then go on to provide readers with guidance designed to help them navigate safely and effectively through these experiences.

The rationale for using a semiotic approach to furnish teachers with guidance on how to deal with these professional hazards has its roots in learning theory. We seem as a species to be driven by a desire to make meanings: to this extent therefore we can be seen as 'homo significans' – meaning-makers. We construct our world and make many of our meanings through our creation and interpretation of 'signs'. A further reason for adopting this approach lies within the theory of constructivism. Constructivism is a psychological theory of knowledge which argues that humans generate knowledge and meaning from their experiences. In this specific case it is highly likely that most beginning teachers will be car drivers and will therefore be familiar with the meanings of many of the road signs used within this book. Even non-driving teachers cannot have failed to notice and question the meanings behind the plethora of signs so evident in our streetscape today. I feel that by utilizing readers' prior knowledge and by providing them with a visual hook in the form of familiar road signs, I will be successful in furnishing them with opportunities to fully internalize the advice and guidance provided for them in this book.

As an educational consultant and ex-professional tutor, I have made numerous local authority and school-based presentations to initial teacher trainees, newly qualified teachers and those teachers who are still in the 'dawn of their careers'. I call this group of teachers 'beginning' teachers. When exploring feedback from these sessions, the need for a book such as this became increasingly evident. Many of these beginning teachers are at a loss to know why they are experiencing behavioural, learning and relational problems with their pupils, when the very same pupils seem to be able to strike up good working relationships with, and behave for, other teachers in the school. What further 'rubs salt into the wounds' is that often the quality of work produced for other teachers by these pupils is of a very high standard. This disparity in pupil behaviour and performance does nothing to address the already fragile self-esteem and confidence of these beginning teachers and helps to create a downward spiral in pupil behaviour, motivation and learning.

The semiotic approach adopted in this book will help to 'signpost' those potentially damaging moments in lessons where the wrong course of action can cause the teacher's plans to go awry, both in terms of pupils' behaviour and their learning. In offering readers a range of possible pre-emptive and reactive strategies, I am confident that this 'downward spiral' in pupils' behaviour, motivation and learning can be avoided.

Introduction

How to use this book

You might like to read this book from cover to cover to get an overall picture of the themes, issues and recommended practices explored in each section. Alternatively, because each section stands on its own, you may wish to turn to a specific page to explore a particular issue that may be relevant to your needs at that time. Whatever strategy you use, I hope that you enjoy your read and that you find the strategies and exemplar scenarios useful.

The book is divided into four sections and a Conclusion. The first part of **Section 1** stresses the importance of knowing **your legal and professional requirements** before you start your teaching journey. It goes on to offer advice for researching the background of your pupils and your new school before providing plenty of tips on getting your classroom, your schemes of work, resources and mindset ready. It draws analogies with your need to check your toolkit, to study your roadmap, to plan your route, to be in a fit condition to travel and to understand the requirements of your teaching journey. Included in this section are all the fundamentals that you need to get to grips with, such as **inspections, reflective practice, EAL students, developing your subject knowledge** and much more.

The aims of **Section 2** are threefold. Using a range of **command signs** as visual prompts the section will 1) explore how these signs could be deemed relevant to teachers' professional scenarios, 2) provide strategies that will help you cope effectively with these scenarios, and 3) provide you with **models of good practice** as a further means of exemplifying this guidance.

The section begins with an exploration of your need to **establish, maintain and reinforce your behaviour and learning expectations** on a consistent basis. It also focuses on the importance of you making an early and positive impression with your classes, before going on to stress your need to set firm learning and behaviour parameters. Following on from this, the section offers you a range of strategies designed to **inject pace and purpose into your lessons**. So what happens when, despite putting these strategies into place, you encounter problems with pupils who simply refuse to carry out your instructions? This section offers you a range of strategies designed to empower you as a teacher and to help you to realize your expectations while at the same time allowing the pupil to retain his or her sense of dignity.

Those of you who have already worked with **teaching assistants (TAs)** will know that, provided their skills and qualities are utilized appropriately, they can be an absolute godsend in lessons. However, the degree to which you are able to use your TAs to make a positive contribution to learning depends very much on the quality of your relationships with these colleagues. This section explores ways in which you can establish and maintain effective working relationships with your TAs, and how you can maximize their use in order to improve learning in the classroom.

Many of you in the secondary phase of education will already be form tutors or are certainly likely to be so at some point in your careers. Primary phase teachers are likely to have responsibility for a single class throughout the academic year. This section explores the ways in which you can create a sense of **ownership of your form/classroom** and how you can use this to establish a sense of safety and security for your pupils.

The final part of this section explores the role of **brain-based learning** and offers a wide range of strategies and activities designed to cater for the various parts of the brain. Advice and guidance are offered on how to plan lessons with pupils' learning styles and intelligence types in mind. Particular emphasis is given to 'starter' activities.

The aims of **Section 3** are again threefold. Using a range of **warning signs** as visual prompts, the section will 1) explore how these signs could be used to warn teachers of potential learning and behaviour hazards, 2) provide a range of proactive strategies designed to reduce these hazards, and 3) provide **models of good practice** that further exemplify this guidance.

Section 3 starts off by offering support to form tutors and/or class teachers on how to integrate new pupils into the class. The issue of **pupil 'labelling'** is explored in some detail before the section goes on to list the ways in which you can use your pupils to induct new colleagues into the class.

A substantial part of this section is given over to examining the need for teachers to be proactive when planning for behaviour management. It is in this section that I introduce the term **'watershed moments'** as a way of describing those points along the planning and teaching continuum where important decisions need to be made about whether or not to take action. As well as looking at possible ways in which to deal with the misdemeanours of individual pupils, a great deal of attention is given to exploring ways in which to manage the really **'challenging class'**.

Good teachers are those who use their **emotional intelligence** to inform their planning, teaching and relationships with pupils. In addition to this they understand the emotional needs of their pupils. This section explores the issue of pupil self-esteem and motivation before going on to demonstrate the link between pupils' thinking processes and the way in which they react to the learning and relationship scenarios presented to them. Much of this book is dedicated to providing advice and guidance on how to establish and maintain good working relationships with your pupils. Although there are some of you who are better at this than others, there is no teacher alive who has not experienced some degree of conflict with the pupils in their classes. It is at this point in the section that I offer substantial advice on how to use your emotional intelligence to 'repair' and 'rebuild' your relationships with these pupils. The final part of the section explores a range of strategies designed to reduce whole-class noise levels when pupils are working on tasks and activities.

Section 4 is dedicated to exploring the links between **direction, information and distance signs** and teaching and learning scenarios. Using these types of road signs as visual prompts, the section explores how keeping pupils informed and providing them with clear guidance about the tasks and activities ahead of them can impact positively on their learning. The importance of sharing learning journeys and objectives when launching schemes of work and/or lessons is stressed within this section.

In addition to this, the section explores the effects of the ever-increasing demands made upon teachers and suggests ways in which you can **control your work load and reduce your stress levels**. Because part of the solution might be to seek help from sympathetic colleagues, this section of the book explores ways in which you can do so while at the same time maintaining your integrity and self-esteem.

Using the 'No-Through Road' sign, this section carries out an in-depth exploration of how to avoid being 'pushed into a corner' by your pupils. It explores the use of 'tactical pausing', 'choice-direction' and 'take-up time' as strategies to establish and maintain control over your pupils in a non-aggressive manner.

The final part of this section relates to your need to fully involve parents in the teaching and learning process. It offers a gamut of advice on how to conduct teacher/parent interviews in the form of formal parents' consultation sessions and how to make more informal contact with parents via the telephone or by letter.

The Conclusion summarizes the key principles of the book before making suggestions about the possible ways forward for you as teachers. I use this chapter to suggest ways in which you too can adopt a semiotic approach towards your teaching by using signs and symbols as learning tools in your lessons. I also ask you to think about ways in which you can demonstrate your understanding of the **hidden curriculum** by making use of signs and symbols to communicate messages about your expectations of, and aspirations for, the pupils in your classes. The conclusion briefly explores the potential for professional tutors, school mentors and trainers of **using a semiotic approach** in the training and mentoring of colleagues.

Section 1

Studying the map and planning your route

Imagine this scenario. You've just passed your driving test, you've got your own car and all you want to do is to get out on to that open road. The last thing you want to do is to read the vehicle manual or to think about whether there is any air in the tyres or whether there is enough water in the cooling system. You are itching to drive round to your friends and family so that you can celebrate your success with your nearest and dearest. Hopefully, as the novelty of learning to drive wears off, you will start to think more responsibly about how to maintain your vehicle and plan your journeys.

Before you start any long journey you are well advised to prepare thoroughly for the road ahead. You need to make sure that your car is road worthy, that each part is in good working order, and that you are clear about how to get to your destination. When using a motor vehicle, it is important to make sure that your documentation is up to date; that you have a legal MOT certificate and tax and insurance documents, and that you have a map or a satellite navigation system in your car. Failure to do this may result in a great deal of expense, inconvenience and stress. The same excitement, spirit of adventure and the eventual adoption of a more 'cautious approach' are true of your journey through your teaching career. Failure to do the groundwork before you start teaching can have serious ramifications for you, your colleagues and most important of all, your pupils. The purpose of this initial section is to provide you with advice and guidance on the preparatory work you need to do *before* you start teaching your classes. Mundane as this process might seem, carrying out these initial tasks can make your professional life and the lives of your pupils that much more secure, successful and free of stress.

The guidance in this section has been presented in order of its significance to you as a beginning teacher. In other words, things that you need to know about as a matter of urgency have been covered in the early part of the section. Less imminent issues can be found towards the end of the section.

Find out about the school and pupils you will be teaching.

1 Your legal and professional requirements

Every Child Matters

Despite the stress and worry of embarking on a new career or starting at a new school, it is important for you to remember that at the very heart of the teaching and learning process is the child. It is because of this that I have selected the **Every Child Matters** or **ECM** agenda as my initial focus for discussion. ECM is a UK government initiative that was launched in 2003, and is one of the most important policy initiatives and development programmes in relation to children and children's services of the last decade. Described as a sea change to the children and families agenda it has been the title of three government papers and led to the Children Act of 2004 (http://publications.everychildmatters.gov.uk/eOrderingDownload/CM5860.pdf).

It's important to remember that every child does, in fact, matter.

Every Child Matters covers children and young people up to the age of 19. Its main aims are for every child, whatever their background or their circumstances, to have the support they need to:

- be healthy;
- stay safe;
- enjoy and achieve;
- make a positive contribution;
- achieve economic wellbeing.

To achieve these outcomes, children need to feel loved and valued, and be supported by a network of reliable and affectionate relationships (HMSO, 2006: 31). If children are denied the opportunities to meet these outcomes

Children need a
balanced and
healthy life at
home and at
school.

and/or the support required to do so, they are at increased risk of an impoverished childhood which in turn can lead to social exclusion in adulthood.

Each of the themes described above has a detailed outcomes framework attached to it that requires multi-agency partnerships to work together to achieve them. These include children's centres, early years, schools, children's social work services, primary and secondary health services, playwork, and Child and Adolescent Mental Health Services (CAMHS). In the past it has been argued that children and families have received poorer services because of the failure of professionals to understand each other's roles and to work together effectively in a multidisciplinary manner. ECM seeks to change this, stressing that it is important for all professionals working with children to be aware of the contribution that could be made by their own and each others' service, and to plan and deliver their work with children and young people accordingly. It is now in place in all schools throughout the United Kingdom and it is the central goal of Every Child Matters to ensure that every pupil is given the chance to be able to work towards the goals referenced within it.

Adopt a multi-
agency approach.
Be clear about
the roles of
colleagues
outside the
teaching
profession.

The implications of ECM for schools are enormous. The ECM agenda needs to be embedded within the institution's formal and hidden curriculum. Subject staff need to plan for the various elements of ECM when devising schemes of work or lesson plans, and pastoral staff need to be fully aware of the legislation, policies and protocols required to keep pupils safe and secure. Although it is important for me to make these particular points, I need to make it clear that it is not within the remit of this book to fully explore the broader school implications of the ECM agenda. It is sufficient for you to know that you need to give every consideration to the ECM when planning your modules of work or your individual lessons.

Incorporate
elements of ECM
into your lesson
planning and
pastoral care.

Safeguarding children

The Children's Act of 2004 requires each local authority to establish a local Safeguarding Children Board (SCB). The SCB is the key statutory mechanism for agreeing how the relevant organizations in each local area will cooperate to safeguard and promote the welfare of children and for ensuring the effectiveness of what they do. The SCB contributes to the wider goals of improving the wellbeing of all children but has particular focus on the 'staying safe' outcome of Every Child Matters.

> Be aware of safeguarding legislation.

You need to be aware of your responsibility as part of the school community to recognize and identify abuse of the pupils within your charge, and of your need to notify the designated person responsible for safeguarding children. For those children who are suffering, or are at risk of suffering harm, joint working is essential to safeguard the child(ren) or young people. Teachers, along with other professionals and agencies, should:

> You will need to recognize signs of abuse in your pupils.

- be alert to potential indicators of abuse or neglect;
- be alert to the risks that individual abusers, or potential abusers, may pose to children and young people;
- share and help to analyse information so that an informed assessment can be made of the child's/young person's needs and circumstances;
- contribute to whatever actions are needed to safeguard the child or young person and promote his or her welfare;
- take part in regularly reviewing the outcomes for children and young people against specific plans;
- work cooperatively with parents, unless this is inconsistent with the need to ensure the child's or young person's safety. (HMSO, 2006: 34, 1.17)

To assist inexperienced beginning teachers, Table 1.1 contains a list of warning signs and indicators. It is reproduced from Suffolk County Council, 2009) with the Council's kind permission.

Table 1.1 Signs and indicators

NEGLECT	EMOTIONAL ABUSE	PHYSICAL ABUSE	SEXUAL ABUSE
■ Tired/listless	■ Clingy	■ Unexplained injuries	■ Age inappropriate sexual behaviour/ knowledge/promiscuity
■ Unkempt	■ Attention seeking	■ Injuries on certain parts of the body	
■ Poor hygiene	■ Over read to relate to others	■ Injuries in various stages of healing	■ Wary of adults/running away from home
■ Untreated medical conditions	■ Low self-esteem	■ Injuries that reflect an artice used	■ Eating disorders/ depression/self harm
■ Hungry	■ Apathy	■ Flinching when approached	■ Unexplained gifts/ money
■ Over eats when food is available	■ Fearful/withdrawn	■ Reluctant to change	
■ Poor growth	■ Sleep disorders	■ Crying/instability	
■ Poor/late attendance	■ Depression/self harm	■ Afraid of home	
	■ Drink/drug/solvent abuse	■ Behavioural extremes	
		■ Apathy/depression	

Reproduced from the 'Introduction to Safeguarding' Delegate workbook
August 2009 with kind permission from Suffolk County Council

As a beginning teacher, it is really tempting to withhold information given to you by a pupil in confidence. It is flattering to think that this pupil has trusted you enough to furnish you with his or her inner thoughts and fears and to give you information that illustrates that something untoward is going on in his or her life. I need to stress that holding on to information is not the way to ensure that children and young people are safeguarded. It is essential that you pass this information on to the right person in your school so that he or she can investigate the issue further. So, how can you do this without damaging your relationship with the pupil and without losing their trust? One of the things I say to young people who confide in me is something like this:

> *I am really pleased that you felt you could come and tell me about this issue and it is really nice to think that you have confided in me. However, you need to know that I am obliged to pass this information on to someone in the school who will be able to offer you advice. You have trusted me enough to tell me about this issue; what I am now asking you to do is to trust me enough to find the right person to deal with this issue in a sympathetic and kind manner.*

At this point it is best not to discuss the issue any further, but if the pupil wants to continue talking, allow him or her to do so, making sure that you do not ask any 'leading questions'. Having said this, it is perfectly acceptable to use active listening techniques to obtain a full account of the issue; these are described in more detail when exploring the 'Repair and Rebuild' process in Section 3. If you do not understand what the pupil has said, simply repeat his or her words with a puzzled look – this is likely to prompt further explanation. If this does not happen, do not push the pupil to say more. The less you say the better. Do not tell the pupil that 'everything will be alright' because it may not be. In short, do not make promises you cannot keep. As soon as the conversation has ended, and after the pupil has left you, write down the general gist of the conversation, making note of the salient points. Make sure that you date and sign the document before you present it to the senior member of staff who has the 'safeguarding' brief in the school.

> Make sure you know who is responsible for 'safeguarding' in your school.

> Don't ask pupils leading questions, but you can use neutral prompts.

2 Researching your pupils' and the school's backgrounds

Inclusion

In order to fully engage all your pupils in the learning process, you need to be aware of what is meant by the term 'inclusion'. According to the Centre of Studies in Inclusive Education website (http://inclusion.uwe.ac.uk/csie/csiefaqs.htm) inclusion in education involves:

- valuing all pupils and staff equally;
- increasing the participation of pupils in, and reducing their exclusion from, the cultures, curricula and communities of local schools;
- restructuring the cultures, policies and practices in schools so that they respond to the diversity of pupils in the locality;
- reducing barriers to learning and participation for all pupils, not just those with impairments or those who are categorized as 'having special educational needs';
- learning from attempts to overcome barriers to the access and participation of particular pupils to make changes for the benefit of pupils more widely;
- viewing the differences between pupils as resources to support learning, rather than as problems to be overcome;
- acknowledging the right of pupils to an education in their locality;
- improving schools for staff as well as for pupils;
- emphasizing the role of schools in building community and developing values, as well as in increasing achievement;
- fostering mutually sustaining relationships between schools and communities.

> You need to plan your lessons to include all pupils irrespective of gender, physical/academic ability, ethnicity or religion.

What this means in practice is that children and young people with physical, social and special education needs (SEN) and those who are able-bodied should now be able to learn together in all educational establishments and be provided with appropriate networks of support. Inclusion means enabling pupils to participate in the life and work of mainstream institutions to the best of their abilities, whatever their needs.

Working with SEN pupils

It is absolutely crucial that you keep up to date with the changes that regularly occur to the **SEN Code of Practice**. You can find a copy of this document at www.teachernet.gov.uk/docbank/index.cfm?id=3724.

> Know your school's SEN policy. Find out about your pupils from the SENCO.

Your school will probably have used this document when creating its own SEN policy but it is important to note that each school will give the document its own flavour. You would be well advised to make sure that you meet with the special needs coordinator (SENCO) to discuss the characteristics of each of your SEN pupils. Although some schools allocate their SEN pupils with a code that highlights the individual pupil's general areas of need (autism, dyslexia, dyspraxia, ADHD, diabetes, asthma, epilepsy, serious food allergies, etc), and although it is very important to enter the code into your mark book, it is vital that you do not rely on the code alone. Experience shows me that although pupils may have similar conditions these are often manifested by pupils in different ways. In addition to needing to gain first-hand knowledge of the expected behaviour patterns of your own individual SEN pupils, you also need to seek the advice of the SENCO about the best ways to simplify the work for these pupils.

As it is not possible to explore every SEN condition, I have provided some generalized guidance that may help to support the learning and inclusion of the SEN pupils in your classes. Important as this guidance is, there is no substitute for discussing the backgrounds of your pupils with your SENCO.

Top tips for teaching SEN pupils

- Make sure that you have read the pupils' **Individual Education Plans (IEPs)**.
- Offer non-threatening but nevertheless challenging tasks and activities.
- Provide a range of opportunities for these pupils to demonstrate what they know and what they can do. This could be through the use of drama, artwork, poetry, storyboards, cartoons, flow diagrams, bullet point lists, word association, diagrams, zones of relevance diagrams, puzzles, true/false quizzes, games, etc.
- Set differentiated learning objectives to allow these pupils to succeed.
- Make sure that you demonstrate or model your learning outcomes. SEN pupils need to know exactly what they are expected to do.
- Ensure that you provide a strong context for the learning. SEN pupils, more than most, need to see the relevance of the work being covered.
- Provide continuity but avoid 'run-over' lessons – this only confuses these pupils.
- Give your SEN pupils short, structured tasks.
- Provide clear written instructions in bullet point fashion.
- Always support your text with visual images such as pictures or video clips.
- Ensure frequent repetition of keywords, subject content or concepts.
- Get your worksheets checked for readability by your SEN coordinator.
- Ensure pupils' access to ICT as this helps them to re-draft their work and improve their presentation.
- Ensure that new vocabulary is recorded and tested on a regular basis.
- Make sure that the assessment reflects the pupils' learning and does not discriminate by structure or language.

Use these top tips to plan your lessons.

- Provide your SEN pupils with a lot of one-to-one contact, either with you or with your teaching assistant(s).
- Promote high self-esteem by overtly valuing every pupil's contribution.
- Liaise with the form tutors of your SEN pupils on pastoral matters.

From Dixie 2009a and b, 'Working with SEN pupils'.

Know your school's EAL (English as an Additional Language) policy. Find out about your pupils from the individual responsible for EAL issues.

In the spirit of true 'inclusive' practice, you need to provide appropriate learning opportunities for those pupils for whom English language is not their mother tongue. To this end therefore, it is important to familiarize yourself with your school's **EAL policy** and use this newly acquired knowledge and understanding to inform your lesson planning.

In the early stages of your practice, try to involve these members of staff in the lesson planning process. Ask them if they can provide you with any resources to support the learning of these pupils. It is important that when you come to record pupils' current levels of achievement, you include an additional column in your mark book for their specific levels in English.

Just as all English-speaking pupils have their own individual learning needs, so too do EAL pupils. Unfortunately, there is a tendency by many to assume that because EAL pupils struggle with the use of fluent English, they are cognitively deficient. It is crucial that you remember that the fluency of EAL pupils in speaking, reading and writing English does not necessarily reflect their cognitive ability. Be very careful not to create a 'one size fits all' model of provision for these pupils. Having said this, it is fair to say that there are certain generalized principles involved in the teaching of EAL pupils, and with this in mind I have provided you with the following top tips.

Top tips for teaching EAL pupils

- Make sure that you carry out some basic research into the cultural and personal backgrounds of the EAL pupils in your classes.
- Ensure that these pupils are comfortable in the classroom. Have them seated in front of you so that they can easily access pictures and texts and where it is easier for you to make regular eye contact with them.
- Ensure that you start each lesson by explaining the key vocabulary being used. Make sure you provide your EAL pupils with a visual version of the glossary of terms to put into their books.
- As far as possible allow each EAL pupil to sit next to a reliable pupil who can act as a translator.
- Identify any cultural content that may be unfamiliar to your EAL pupils and be prepared to explain this, perhaps drawing parallels with other cultures.
- Make sure that you repeat and summarize instructions and requests, but be very careful not to vary your language too much when you repeat yourself as this might result in the pupil spending unnecessary time working out if there are any differences between the two messages. Moderate your speed of delivery to meet the needs of these pupils.
- Wherever possible give practical demonstrations to your EAL pupils. Supporting your words with actions is a highly effective way of conveying a message to them. However, you do need to be highly sensitive to the fact that body language and gestures vary in meaning between cultures. In many cultures children are taught to avoid making eye contact with their elders. A thumbs-up gesture in Britain, for example, symbolizes encouragement. In Bangladesh it is the equivalent of the two-finger sign.
- If you are a teacher of English, use dual textbooks where possible.
- If there is a bilingual teacher in the school who can help you, get him or her to produce worksheets in the pupil's own language.

Use these top tips to plan your lessons.

- Do not over-correct the mistakes of your EAL pupils as this will soon cause them to become demotivated. Have a specific focus when assessing pupils' work and when setting targets.
- When you are correcting the written work of your EAL pupil, use the same colour as the pupil has used.
- Encourage risk-taking within a safe and secure environment. Create a can-do culture within the classroom and have high expectations of your EAL pupils. Expect them to succeed.
- When providing work for EAL pupils make sure that you differentiate. For example, single-word answers are acceptable from a pupil who is new to English but, with increasing experience, pupils must be encouraged to expand their answers and use full sentences.
- Find opportunities to use role play and drama.
- Make use of writing frames but only if pupils have had the opportunity to talk through their work prior to the written task.

From Dixie 2009.

Researching and exploring the school and its environs

Much of the guidance offered within this section is based on the assumption that you will be starting at a new school. Having said this, I do believe that the teaching and learning of experienced and long-standing teachers would benefit from reappraising themselves with current initiatives, with the school's internal documentation and with the roles of key personnel. The pressures of everyday school life are such that many teachers tend to work in insular fashion, perhaps every now and again reaching out to make contact with those people whose roles impact directly upon their daily work. It would certainly benefit pupil learning if staff could explore the roles of others and work in a more collaborative manner.

Although I would strongly advise that you read and inwardly digest your school's prospectus, I would urge you to do this with a 'critical eye'. This document is likely to maintain that all members of staff share the norms and values of their institution and that each and every person in the school is 'singing from the same hymn sheet' and is fully valued by the senior management team. However, all you have to do is to visit a range of lessons or walk the corridors to see that massive incongruities and inconsistencies occur in our schools. It is important that you spend some time in your school making an assessment of the quality of relationships between teaching and non-teaching staff, as these can often indicate whether the school acts as a corporate body, or whether there is any divisiveness in the system. I would urge you to give full consideration to the list of questions provided below that are designed to test the 'relationship waters' in schools:

> Find out about the quality of relationships in the school.

- Is there a 'them and us' situation in the staffroom?
- Are non-teaching personnel invited to staff meetings?
- Are non-teaching personnel offered full opportunities for professional development?
- Are non-teaching personnel afforded the same status when implementing the school's behaviour management policy?
- Do teachers share their lesson plans and learning objectives with teaching assistants? (Dixie, 2009a: 41)

The rationale behind providing you with these questions is that as 'beginning' teachers you need as much help and support as possible. It is vital to involve and fully respect the contributions made by the non-teaching staff in your school. They are often a source of important information about the pupils and can provide you with support with both pupil learning and behaviour. Further guidance as to how to use classroom teaching assistants, behaviour support staff, etc is provided on page 105 in Section 2.

Exploring the catchment area

Whether you are new to the school or not, I would always strongly advise that you acclimatize yourself with its local environs. A quick tour around

> **Look at your school's catchment area to find out about the socio-economic status of the families of your pupils.**

the area will give you a good indication of the socio-economic make up of the families living in the catchment area and will help you to identify the type of support you may need to offer some of the pupils in your classes. Take a drive around the catchment area at break and/or lunchtime to identify the key meeting areas for pupils, who should officially be confined to the school grounds. It is also a really good idea to get chatting to pupils about what's going on in the neighbourhood. Doing this will allow you to identify potential 'hot spots' for pupil misdemeanours and/or conflict with local residents. Having this local knowledge will help you to track down challenging pupils in the event of them leaving the school site.

At this point I am aware that I have painted a somewhat bleak picture of schools. Please do not be too concerned about this – most pupils in most schools will stick to the rules about staying on site, but good teachers will always hold a realistic view of the youngsters in their charge.

Exploring the hidden curriculum

Having taught in both the primary and secondary sector, and having visited numerous schools in my role as an educational consultant, I am confident in stating that every school has its own distinct culture, ethos and atmosphere. Combined, these provide the visitor, and more importantly the pupils, teachers and corporate staff, with a strong indication of its norms, values and expectations. I have been invited into schools that have simply 'left me cold'. Buildings are shoddy, displays are damaged, poorly constructed or simply non-existent and there is sense of negative determinism about the place. Conversely, I have visited schools where great efforts have been made to keep the school litter-free, where displays have been laminated or placed behind protective sheeting, and where there is a real sense of optimism in the air.

The set of informal and unofficial messages that is relayed to pupils by the culture of a school is known to educationalists as the 'hidden curriculum'. I stress the need for teacher trainees to take great heed of the hidden curriculum in their practice schools, as it can go a long way to informing their relationships with pupils and the quality of their learning. I define the hidden curriculum as follows:

> The hidden curriculum is a combined set of values, attitudes and knowledge frames which are embodied in the organization and processes of schooling and which are implicitly conveyed to pupils. Although all schools have a formal curriculum comprising areas of the academic knowledge which pupils are expected to acquire, it is the form of schooling and the messages transmitted as a result of its organization and practices, which are more powerful than the content of its subjects. It promotes social control and an acceptance of the school's, and hence society's, authority structure. (Dixie 2009a: 39)

As beginning teachers you may understand the term 'hidden curriculum' in generic terms, but you might not yet be fully aware of what it means in practice. To this end therefore, I have provided guidance on some of the relevant aspects of the hidden curriculum that you need to address in preparation for the teaching journey ahead of you.

Relationships within the school

Teacher-pupil relationships lie at the very heart of the learning equation. Whether you are a teacher trainee in your training year, or whether you are in the early years of your teaching career, you need to learn from the practice of others. Keep a watchful eye out for the way in which pupils interact with other teachers during their lessons and in out-of-lesson contexts. Although it is important for you to note the degree to which pupils display respect for their teachers, it is equally important for you to recognize the extent to which this respect is reciprocated, especially when teachers are admonishing pupils. It is very disappointing to see teachers 'laying into' pupils, pointing and wagging their fingers at the miscreants. I find it extremely frustrating that these teachers do not seem to understand that by taking this type of disciplinary action there will be no opportunity for them to 'repair' and 'rebuild' the relationships with these pupils at a later point. Advice and guidance on how to create a restorative climate is offered in Section 3.

> Plan your classroom layout and display with the hidden curriculum in mind.

Brain-based learning

A great deal of attention has been given to brain-based learning over the past five years and quite rightly so. In my opinion anything that helps teachers to understand how pupils learn should be given full credence. This part of the book briefly explores the various functions of the brain before going on to explain how we can use this knowledge to create a positive classroom ethos, to manage our classes and to improve our relationships with pupils.

Dr Paul MacLean of the National Institute of Mental Health in Washington DC purported the theory that suggests that the human brain can be divided into three distinct areas; see Figure 2.1. He named these as:

1   the neo-cortex;
2   the limbic system; and
3   the reptilian brain.

The neo-cortex is divided into two hemispheres and joined by the corpus callosum, which can be found at the top of the brain and which provides a cognitive function. This part of the brain is used to solve problems and to identify patterns. The **limbic system** deals with the emotions, beliefs and value systems, and concerns itself with the long-term memory of the person. However, it is the oldest evolutionary part of the brain – **the reptilian brain** – that provides the main focus for this part of the book. I believe knowledge of the reptilian brain to be of fundamental importance to teachers who are endeavouring to establish, maintain and develop good working relations with their pupils.

The reptilian brain is responsible for routine bodily functions such as breathing, heartbeat, blood pressure and balance. It is the primeval part of the brain that takes charge of our survival responses. The reptilian brain helps us to judge whether to flee or to fight in times of danger. Just as in the animal world, the reptilian brain predisposes us to a system of social conformity, of being able to know one's place in the hierarchy, and of possessing the need to respond to ritualistic rules. In situations where individuals feel threatened, the reptilian brain takes over from the other

The Structure of the Brain

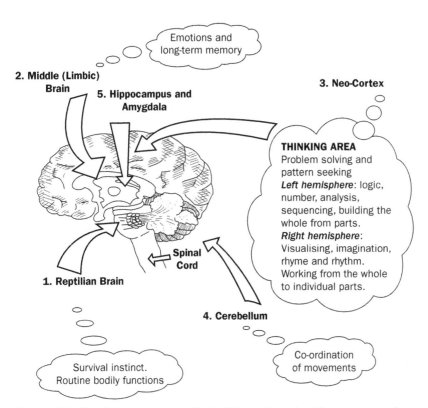

Emotions and long-term memory

2. Middle (Limbic) Brain

5. Hippocampus and Amygdala

3. Neo-Cortex

THINKING AREA
Problem solving and pattern seeking
Left hemisphere: logic, number, analysis, sequencing, building the whole from parts.
Right hemisphere: Visualising, imagination, rhyme and rhythm. Working from the whole to individual parts.

Spinal Cord

1. Reptilian Brain

4. Cerebellum

Survival instinct. Routine bodily functions

Co-ordination of movements

Figure 2.1 The Structure of the Brain (Reproduced with permission from Dixie, 2005)

two areas, and the higher order functions of the brain lose their significance. Having an understanding of the role of the reptilian brain allows us to deal with pupils sympathetically and empathically, especially in challenging 'conflict type' situations where both parties might feel threatened.

Make sure that your pupils have access to water, fresh air and, where possible, natural light.

Labelling

It is important to ascertain whether **'labelling'** is occurring in your lessons. In Dixie (2005) I refer to the work of Rist (1970) and Keddie (1976) who describe the labelling process in some detail, and whose work has informed my practice during my teaching career. Labelling, in an educational sense, is the way in which pupils are encouraged and/or taught to see themselves by their teachers. It is important to note that not all labelling is negative; positive labelling can occur where the self-belief and esteem of pupils are fully enhanced by the teacher through the use of praise and positive motivational language. Negative labelling, however, is a very different 'ball game' and is often carried out overtly by using negative terminology to brand pupils. Pupils are often referred to as being nasty, evil, thick, 'trouble', unlike their siblings, etc. You also need to be aware that negative labelling can be carried out in a more subtle manner. This can manifest itself in the teacher ignoring and/or not challenging specific pupils or groups of pupils within the class, and making the assumption that they are unintelligent or unmotivated.

> Adopt an inclusive approach towards your teaching.

In making an assessment of the hidden curriculum, you will no doubt pick up on the nuances of pupil-teacher relationships in your school(s).

Getting to know your pupils: researching pupils' backgrounds

Teaching is an interactive process that requires an ever-changing system of exchange and negotiation between you and your pupils. It is important for all of us to remember that employing the 'jug and mug' principle, with the children being the empty receptacles into which you simply pour a healthy portion of knowledge, is no longer appropriate. Pupils should no longer be considered as the 'passive recipients' of the teacher's subject knowledge expertise. Pupils bring their own socially constructed agendas into the classroom. These agendas have been formed through their experiences both at home and at school, and manifest themselves in the idiosyncrasies, expectations, aspirations and intentions brought into the school and into your classroom.

It is, therefore, totally understandable that at some point during the working day even the most effective and skilful of teachers will experience a 'conflict of interest' between the values of the school and those of some of the youngsters in their classes. It is your role as teachers to reduce the number of situations that could conflict with your ultimate aim – that of producing effective learning scenarios for pupils. Getting to know pupils is vital if you want to avoid conflict, and if you want your pupils to realize their potential. Gone are the days when teachers were seen as omnipotent beings. In my consultancy role I often come across small 'pockets of staff' who, despite being unsuccessful with their behaviour management and working relationships with pupils, are still very reluctant to alter their practice. When delivering professional development sessions, I use the following statement in an attempt to get these rather intransigent teachers to rethink their practice:

If you always think what you've always thought
You'll always do what you've always done
And if you always do what you've always done
You'll always get what you've always got (Author: Unknown)

So, what exactly is the best way to find out about your pupils? The answer is simple – take the time and trouble to ask them about their lives. Pupils appreciate it when teachers do this, and making time to interview your pupils on a one-to-one basis will most certainly pay off in the long-run. However, if you haven't got the time to do this then it is worth seeking the help of your colleagues. Very often the people with the most up-to-date and detailed background information on your pupils will be the head of year, form tutor and, if relevant, the SENCO. Spend some time talking to them about what makes these pupils tick. I have furnished you with a list of questions which might help you to do this:

- Who are the child's chief carers? Is there a step dad/step mum in the family?
- Does the child have siblings? Do they live in the family home?
- Do siblings go to the same school?
- If the child's biological mother/father does not live in the family home, do they visit/stay with them?

Find out about
your pupils by
asking their
heads of year.

- Are family relationships harmonious? How does the child behave at home?
- Does the child experience any social/emotional/behavioural difficulties? How are these manifested in the classroom? If so, are they getting any support?
- What interests, hobbies, etc does the child have?
- Who are the child's friends at school? How harmonious are these relationships?

Often, simply taking the time and trouble to find out about your pupils is enough to change your relationships with them for the better. Because many youngsters at this stage of their lives feel so confused about their identity and feelings, they often get defensive when interacting with adults. All teachers would be well advised to heed the following two quotes, both of which beautifully illustrate the need for the adolescent to be 'understood':

Sometimes we put up walls, not to block people out but to see who cares enough to tear them down. (Author: Pupil, aged 14)

Adolescence represents an inner emotional upheaval, a struggle between the eternal human wish to cling on to the past and the equally powerful wish to get on with the future.(Louise Kaplan, 1984)

In addition to finding out about the social and emotional backgrounds of your pupils, you will be expected to research and explore their academic backgrounds with a view to using these data to set individual and whole-school targets. One of main sources of information about the social and academic backgrounds of pupils is the **Fischer Family Trust** (http://www.fischertrust.org).

The Fischer Family Trust (FFT) is an independent, non-profit-making organization and a registered charity. It is mainly involved in undertaking and supporting projects addressing the development of education in the UK. A number of analyses are provided by FFT for schools and their local authority to aid self-evaluation. The FFT analyses are distributed to schools via the Assessment Support/Professional Support Teams. In 2005, in conjunction with OfSTED, FFT developed a 'School Self Evaluation Report' (Analyses to Support Self-evaluation), which was first distributed to primary and secondary schools during the 2005 autumn term. OfSTED inspectors may request this report before an inspection takes place, in order for them to start drawing up hypotheses about a school's performance. The report collates data on individual pupil's performance in KS2, KS3 and KS4 tests, and analyses value-added progress over a three-year period; it produces an overview of trends in performance for the school and for groups within it. FFT uses a contextual value-added model throughout these analyses. Reports are not provided for KS1, Infant or Special schools.

Following requests from secondary schools, a split FFT Access database is available to all secondary schools via the Lancashire ROSE website (http://www.lancsngfl.ac.uk/curriculum/assessment/index.php? category_id=95&s=!B29062ef2e1dcee6057f6c2f2df2ed7). This database allows schools to choose from a range of FFT pupil-level and school-level reports and pupil estimates, and then to generate these 'in-house'.

> It is vital to become familiar with the Fischer Family Trust information for the pupils in your classes.

School policies

You will no doubt be aware that it is a legal requirement for all schools to produce their own policy documents on such issues as special educational needs, pupil behaviour, pupil inclusion, equal opportunities, anti-bullying, health and safety, etc. It is highly likely that you will have been presented with these policies when you joined the school staff. However, it is important to note that the sign of a good school is when staff actually put these policies into practice on a daily basis. I have visited a number of schools where the paperwork looks mighty impressive, but where the actions of the staff do not always match the high ideals laid out on the written page.

While on your visit, keep a particular look-out for consistency of approach from all staff on such aspects as managing pupil behaviour and health and safety issues in science, technology, drama and PE lessons. Find out what happens when there is an incident of racism in the school. Do the actions of the school match the recommendations laid out in the policy? To what extent are the opportunities for pupils with special educational needs matched to those laid out in the SEN policy? Make sure that you adopt a critical stance when reviewing the paperwork presented to you. To help you to do this I have provided you with another set of questions (from Dixie, 2009a) to think about:

> Get to know how your school policies work.

- How accessible are these policies to teaching and non-teaching personnel? Have posters and/or summary documents been displayed around the school?
- To what extent do the aims and objectives laid out in these policies reflect the reality of school life?
- To what degree are the *teaching and non-teaching personnel* aware of, and intimate with, the details of these policies? For example, do they know what to do in the event of a pupil making a disclosure to them? Do they know the procedure for reporting a racist incident? Do they know what to do if they suspect that a child is suffering some form of abuse?
- To what degree are the *pupils* aware of, and intimate with, the details of these policies? For example, do they know what to do if *they* are being bullied? Do *they* know the procedure for reporting a racist incident? Are *they* fully aware of the details of the school's behaviour policy?

Extracurricular activities

As an Initial Teacher Training (ITT) tutor I often advise trainees to assess the commitment and drive of the teaching staff in their host schools, by paying a visit to the car park about half an hour after the end of the school day when there are no meetings. I ask them to simply note the number of cars still in the car park. Are they able to detect the smell of burning rubber as dozens of teachers make a hasty retreat from the school premises, or are there a significant number of staff who use this time to referee or umpire sports matches, to run training sessions, drama rehearsals or extracurricular clubs? Most schools will be able to provide an audit of the extracurricular activities that occur at lunchtime or after school, so it is worth having a look at this to make an assessment of the level of commitment of the staff and/or to see whether there is anything you feel you could get involved in. You could use the questions laid below (from Dixie, 2009a) to help your enquiry into this aspect of school life:

Meet your pupils on an informal basis on school trips or at after-school clubs.

- What extracurricular activities and school trips does the school provide?
- Are these activities and trips available and accessible to *all* pupils?
- How aware are the pupils of these activities and trips? Are they publicised?
- Do these extracurricular activities and trips help to improve the quality of the relationships between teachers and pupils? If this is the case, how does this occur?

Assemblies

Functionalist sociologists have long argued that schools can be seen as microcosms of society; that the social conditions prevalent within the workplace and society in general are often deliberately replicated within the school environment. Whether you think that this is a good thing or not is not up for debate, but I am sure you will agree that this is indeed the case. Nowhere is this more obvious than in school assemblies. I strongly advise you to attend the assemblies aimed at a range of year groups and make a careful note of the types of messages being imparted, and of the standard of behaviour exhibited by pupils. Assemblies are often used as a strategy to transmit strong corporate messages to pupils and to engender a sense of 'togetherness' in the school. You need to decide the degree to which your host school is successful in doing this. The following questions (from Dixie, 2009a) might help you to arrive at your decision:

Get your tutor group to make an input into assemblies.

- Are whole-school assemblies delivered?
- How many assemblies does each year group have?

- What strategies are used to establish and maintain social order?
- How well do the pupils behave in assemblies? How attentive are they?
- To what extent are the assemblies used to deliver religious messages?
- To what extent are the assemblies used to deliver humanist messages?
- How successful are the assemblies in helping to transmit the norms and values of the school?

3 Preparing your classroom

Quality of classroom environment and displays

In Dixie (2005) I afford a great deal of attention to the positive messages that can be transmitted to pupils through the medium of effective classroom and corridor displays. If we accept that the hidden curriculum of a school embodies and demonstrates the culture and ethos of a school, then we should accept that classroom and corridor displays are the perfect scenarios with which to do this. To provide real focus to your enquiry into this aspect of school life, I have provided a number of questions (from Bell and Dixie, 2009: 38) for you to consider while you are making your tour of the school:

> Classroom displays can have an extremely positive effect on pupils' learning output and relationships with you.

- What *academic skills* are being transmitted through the medium of classroom/corridor display?
- What *personal qualities* are being transmitted through the medium of classroom/corridor display?
- How do classroom/corridor displays encourage a positive attitude towards work?
- How do classroom/corridor displays encourage a positive attitude towards authority and the school rules?
- How do classroom/corridor displays encourage hard work and productivity?
- How do classroom/corridor displays encourage a respect for others?

Creating a physical environment that provides pupils with adequate light, heat and seating space and the opportunity to drink fluids, will help to make your pupils feel safe, secure, happy and ready to learn. More and more schools are allowing their pupils to drink in class, so you need to find out what the policy is in your school. I am quite happy for pupils to drink juice and water in my lessons, but cola is most definitely banned!

In addition to your need to plan the physical aspects of the learning environment, the emotional conditions of the classroom need to be considered. To do this, you need to reduce scenarios that create anxiety, fear, lack of self-esteem, a feeling of isolation, insecurity and a sense of injustice. In short, you, as the teacher need to reduce pupil stress. My advice to you, as 'beginning' teachers, is to take this information on board when you are planning the physical layout of your classroom. My research reveals that even the most motivated and positive of teachers do not plan their classroom displays with the reptilian brain in mind. You need to be aware that you can do a great deal to cater for the needs of your pupils, even before you start formally teaching them. With that in mind, I have furnished you with a few ideas that will help you to do this.

Encourage healthy risk-taking in lessons.

One of the most important messages for you to get across to your pupils is that it is perfectly acceptable to get things wrong. In the true spirit of humanism, risk-taking is an integral part of the learning process, but this will not happen in a competitive learning environment. To establish a collaborative ethos in the classroom you could produce a number of posters with motivational messages. Allow me to furnish you with an example from my own classroom as described in Dixie (2007). Displayed immediately *opposite* a poster stating that 'It's OK to be Wrong', is a building block model which visually demonstrates the need for my pupils to work together to solve problems.

In the establishment phase, and at regular points throughout the year, I explain to my pupils that each wrong answer given in lessons should be seen as a stimulus (or building block) for other pupils to take the thought process that bit further. In this way, an incorrect response is still given a degree of status! Each partially correct response acts as a building block for other pupils to further develop their thought patterns, and brings the class that bit closer to the desired outcome. I emphasize to the pupils that the process should be seen as collaborative and not individualistic. I have to say that using this approach has had a dramatic effect on my relationships with my pupils. Pupils are more willing to get involved, talk to me,

It's OK to be wrong!

ask questions and, most important, are more prepared to 'take risks' in lessons. So, why exactly does this happen? I would propose that this happens simply because they do not feel threatened. In Dixie (2007) I emphasize how using this particular model can also help to dramatically reduce discipline problems in lessons.

Simply putting up posters in the classroom encouraging pupils to 'take risks', can provide the pupils with a sense of security. Explaining to the pupils that you will always be there to 'catch them if they fall' helps to provide them with the security net they need to take those risks so vital to their academic and social development. I feel that the following quote from a Year 10 pupil really captures the flavour of what I am trying to say.

When I arrived in the classroom, I felt insecure, but as I settled and looked around, I saw many pictures, posters and signs which help me to understand what is involved by being in the class. Pupils feel shy when they put their hands up, just in case they get it wrong. But in this class there are signs that say 'Take a risk' so it is much easier and less threatening when there is something telling you to take a risk and put your hand up. (Dixie, 2005: 75)

Again in line with a humanist perspective on learning, I believe that it is important for youngsters to realize that making mistakes is part of the learning process. To this end therefore, you need to inform them that you are doing your best to provide an environment where they feel comfortable in showing their vulnerabilities. The internet is a great source of motivational quotes. I displayed these two traditional Chinese proverbs in my classroom to get over the notion of using failure as a means to success:

Failure lies not in falling down but in not getting up. (Traditional)

Good people are good because they've come to wisdom through failure. (William Saroyan, 1908–1981)

> Develop a 'collaborative' climate in your teaching room. Empower your pupils by making yours a 'can do' classroom.

I am sure you will agree that raising the self-esteem of pupils has got to be a major aim of any committed teacher. To my mind you need to make this message overt! Simply pegging up the following message on a washing line can be really effective:

THIS IS A 'CAN DO' CLASSROOM

Although this message is pretty basic it is nevertheless very effective. The following observation made by a Year 10 pupil about the culture of this classroom makes my point well:

When you walk into the room all the work on the walls shows that it is a hardworking room. The first banner on the wall – 'This is a Can

Do classroom' – shows that the teacher is enthusiastic and wants us to do well. All the displays have obviously had a lot of work put into them and this tells us the teacher works hard to create a good working atmosphere. (Pupil aged 14; from Dixie, 2005: 77)

It is also important that you convey to your pupils that they do their best in your lessons. Again, do not worry about making your message too obvious. Setting the scene by displaying motivational posters, such as the one shown below, goes a long way to getting across to your pupils exactly what you expect of them. Providing pupils with firm expectations and clear parameters can help to cater for the reptilian brain:

> Use primary colours to decorate your class.

Never underestimate the use of primary colours and creative displays in promoting warmth and purpose in your classroom. Bright reds, complemented by an array of green plants for example, can go a long way to creating a purposeful and stimulating atmosphere, and can convey to the pupils that they are here to work. This is exemplified in the following quotes from Year 10 pupils (from Dixie, 2005: 78):

> *When I enter the classroom first thing in the morning, I feel a sudden sense of security. Everywhere I look there is advice and information to help me through my work. The room also has a natural side to it with the plants in the corner and I like that feeling in a classroom. I prefer a classroom which makes a person feel good.* (Pupil aged 14)

> *When I enter this room, I feel very welcome. There are many colourful posters and motivational quotes. It makes me feel comfortable and willing to work. If the teacher has put in a great deal of effort making this room welcoming, I feel I must put in a great deal of effort into the work he sets me.* (Pupil aged 14)

> *This classroom makes me feel welcome and because a lot of effort and time have been put into it I will put effort and time into my work. It makes me motivated and gives the teacher respect as well as gives the room respect.* (Pupil aged 14)

Careers and work-experience opportunities

Many secondary schools provide opportunities for careers education through the formal curriculum and/or the medium of **personal social and health education (PSHE).** Most schools however, provide vocational advice and guidance in more informal manner through the hidden curriculum. Having said this, it is important to note the increased vocational input into school life with the advent of the **14–19 Curriculum.** While you are in your schools, take an opportunity to talk to pupils about the quality of careers guidance offered. Make sure that you do this across a range of year groups. Visit the careers room to have a look at the wall displays and to ascertain the quality of the resources offered to the pupils. Talk to the work-experience coordinator about the opportunities offered to older pupils and about the vocational opportunities provided for 'challenging' pupils lower down the school. Here is a range of questions (from Dixie, 2009) for you to consider when exploring this issue:

- Does vocational education form part of the school's timetable? If so, how many hours per week are allocated to careers-related issues?
- To what extent are vocational issues promoted around the school through the medium of wall displays?
- Does the school have a careers adviser?
- Does the school have a careers room? How comprehensive is the information provided? Does the school have a work-experience programme? Is this available to all pupils?
- Does the school have links with the vocational departments in local colleges? To what extent do they work together to provide opportunities for the pupils in the school?

> Take your class to the careers room during registrations.

4 Exploring the OfSTED report

OfSTED is an independent inspectorate that reports directly to parliament. It inspects and regulates institutions in England that provide education to learners of all ages, and also inspects providers of care for children and young people. The Education and Training Inspectorate in Northern Ireland, Her Majesty's Inspectorate of Education in Scotland, and Estyn in Wales perform similar functions within their education systems. From 2011, the inspection will focus on four aspects of school life: pupil achievement; the quality of teaching; leadership and management; and the behaviour and safety of pupils. In a way this is very much like an MOT inspection for schools. Just as you would need to ascertain whether a motor vehicle is safe and 'fit for purpose', the same process needs to be carried out for schools.

Until recently, every school has been required to complete a lengthy Self-Evaluation Form (SEF), designed to get them to explore their strengths and weaknesses, and to use in setting targets. The 2010 White Paper *The Importance of Teaching* states that, from August 2011, schools will be required to complete a brief 'centralised' document prior to inspection.

The 2011 OfSTED arrangements will adopt a highly proportionate approach to inspection. Since outstanding schools generally have robust systems in place to support their continued excellent performance, routine inspection of schools and sixth form colleges previously judged to be outstanding will cease, and they will only be re-inspected if there is evidence of decline or widening attainment gaps. The same principle is also expected to apply to outstanding special schools and PRUs.

The weaker the school, the more frequent the monitoring will be: schools judged to be inadequate will receive termly monitoring visits to assess improvement. In order to help with this proportional approach, OfSTED will differentiate within the broad 'satisfactory' category, between schools which are improving and have good capacity to improve further, and schools that are stuck. Schools that are satisfactory but making little progress will be more likely to receive a monitoring visit from OfSTED within the year, and may be judged inadequate if they have not improved. Where a school feels that its last OfSTED judgement is out of date and does not reflect the improvement it has made since its last inspection, it should be able to request an inspection. After every inspection OfSTED publishes the report on its website.

Special measures

'**Special measures**' is a status applied by OfSTED and Estyn to schools assessed as failing to supply an acceptable level of education and which appear to lack the leadership necessary to secure improvements. A school subject to special measures will have regular short-notice OfSTED inspections to monitor its improvement. The senior managers and teaching staff can be dismissed, and the school governors replaced by an appointed executive committee. If poor performance continues, the school may be closed. The current circumstances under which a school may be placed in special measures, and the procedures to follow, are stipulated by the Education Act 2005. Prior to 2005, special measures were applied to any school that was failing to supply an acceptable level of education; potential for improvement under current leadership was not taken into account. Under the new rules, schools demonstrating such potential are given a notice to improve and re-inspected after one year.

Once an institution has been placed in special measures, it is presented with an action plan by the inspectors detailing the key areas it needs to develop in order to leave the category. Monitoring of this action plan then passes to HMI (Her Majesty's Inspectors) who visit the school typically once a term for one to two days to evaluate progress. Once HMI are satisfied that the action plan has been completed, and all points satisfactorily addressed, they will refer the school back to OfSTED and ask it to schedule a second Section 5 Inspection. If OfSTED agrees with HMI's judgement, the school is then removed from the special measures category. It is important to note that if a school in special measures fails to improve within a year it is invited to consider becoming an academy. Support for schools that enter special measures comes in a variety of forms, and varies from local authority to local authority. Schools will normally benefit from significant extra resources, both in terms of extra funds and consultancy from the local authority and external providers.

If you are a trainee, you are highly unlikely to be observed or interviewed by an OfSTED inspector but you do need to know that there will be implications for you during this time. It is important that you keep a heightened awareness of the stressful nature of an OfSTED inspection and bear this in mind when making demands on your colleagues. The three days given to schools as notice of an inspection are usually spent in a frenetic manner by teaching and non-teaching staff. The prime aim for these staff over the three days will be to get their paperwork up-to-date, to make the school look as attractive as possible and to produce imaginative and enjoyable lessons for the pupils. Whatever your views on the efficacy and/or morality of what you see going on around you, you do need to be aware that this is a very vulnerable and stressful time for most teaching and non-teaching staff.

If you are an NQT or relatively new teacher, you will obviously feel the impact of an OfSTED inspection far more than the trainees in your school. As a full member of the corporate school staff you stand a reasonable chance of being observed or interviewed by the inspectors.

> Make sure that all your records are up to date.

If you decide to apply for a job at a new school it is always advisable to become fully acquainted with its most recent OfSTED report. There are two reasons for this: first, because it is a good idea to be informed about the strengths and weaknesses of your potential workplace; second, because displaying knowledge of these characteristics in your letter of application and at your interview will show that you have taken the trouble to carry out research into the school. This will almost certainly place you in good light as far as the interview panel is concerned.

5 Lesson planning and preparing your resources

Schemes of work, lesson planning and resources

A **scheme of work** defines the structure and content of a course. It maps out clearly how resources (eg books, equipment, time), class activities (teacher-talk, group work, practical sessions, discussions, etc) and assessment strategies (eg tests, quizzes, Q&A, homework) will be used to ensure that the learning aims and objectives of the course are met. The scheme of work has usually been produced as an interpretation of a specification or syllabus, and can be used as a guide throughout the course to monitor progress against the original plan. It is always advisable that schemes of work be shared with pupils so that they have an overview of their journey throughout the course. The typical content for a scheme of work is:

- subject knowledge;
- differentiated objectives and outcomes;
- methods of delivery (student and teacher activity);
- assessment strategies;
- resources.

Continuing with the analogy of the road journey, the scheme of work is the large-scale map the teacher uses to plot the learning journey from point A to point B. Having said this, the journey itself should not be set in stone and the scheme of work should not be considered as being immutable but as a fluid working document. To this end the document should be regularly annotated before then being revised on a yearly basis. It is the most useful evaluation tool you can have, because given that most of us

> A scheme of work should be written in enough detail to allow another member of staff to use it to teach their pupils.

repeat courses year upon year, and that new cohorts of pupils may well have differing needs, referring to previous schemes is the best way to improve your teaching and pupils' learning.

So what is the difference between **lesson plans** and schemes of work? The difference is simply one of scale: whereas the scheme of work is the large-scale plan for the duration of the course, the lesson plan is produced on a much smaller scale, is more detailed and looks at what you are going to do within a relatively limited period of time. (Some people even put timings, minute-by-minute, in their lesson plans.) The point of a lesson plan is to guide you in organizing yourself and your material with the ultimate purpose of helping your pupils to achieve the intended learning outcomes.

> A well planned lesson can challenge pupils of all abilities and dramatically reduce the number of pupils who are off-task and engaging in inappropriate behaviour.

Although I provide an example of a lesson plan on page 45 (also available online at http://education.dixie.continuumbooks.com) you need to be aware that there is no single format for successful lesson planning. Different training organizations and different schools adopt their own planning systems. However, there are a number of key elements that make for good planning. You need to remember that the primary audience for your lesson plan is *you!* Before you start planning your lessons you might like to consider these prompt questions (from Dixie, 2009b):

- What is the purpose of the lesson?
- What are the objectives for the lesson?
- What is the best way for the pupils to achieve?
- What activities or tasks will help them to achieve?
- What is the minimum amount of time needed for each task or activity?
- What will happen when different pupils take different amounts of time to do a task?
- What extension activities can I provide for those pupils who finish their work early?
- Are the pupils likely to be fully occupied in learning throughout the lesson?
- Have I catered for my EAL, SEN and/or G&T pupils?
- How much time do I set aside to settle the class, take the register, introduce the topic, hand out equipment or books, clear up and dismiss the pupils?

- What materials and resources will I need to assemble before the lesson?
- Have I planned homework opportunities for pupils?
- Have I made the learning journey transparent to my teaching assistant?

Exemplar Lesson Plan

Teacher:	Teaching group	Room:
Date:	Time:	TA:

Learning objectives: National Curriculum links: Exam specification links		
SEN pupils: EAL pupils: Differentiation: By the end of the lesson All pupils will .... Most pupils will ... Some pupils will ... TA support will be used to ... Other means of differentiation:		
Context:		
Resources (including ICT):		
Behaviour management issues:		
Health and safety issues:		
ECM:		
Lesson structure		

Teacher activity Starter: Main activities:	Pupil activity

Monitoring and assessment During lesson: After lesson:	
Plenary: Key learning points to be confirmed: Questions to ask:	

Lesson phases

There has been a recent move towards the four-part lesson (Starter, Objectives, Application and Plenary) but I suggest that when you plan your lessons you think about the process as having three discrete phases: an introduction, the main body and the conclusion.

1. Introduction

The introductory phase of the lesson requires you to set out your aims and objectives, perhaps using a 'holding' or 'starter' task to launch the main theme. It is also the part of the lesson that requires you to consolidate and review the learning that has occurred previously and then to make links with new learning scenarios. This phase of the lesson requires you to *introduce* new concepts and content to the pupils, and to put these into context using language they are likely to understand. This is also a good time and place to model examples of good practice as a means of raising pupils' expectations of their performances.

2. Main body

The main phase of the lesson requires you to teach a new body of knowledge/skills, or to provide pupils with an in-depth exploration of concepts, ideas or viewpoints. This is the part of the lesson when you would expect pupils to complete their tasks and activities – in groups, in pairs or on an individual basis. The main body of the lesson should contain a range of activities and should offer opportunities for pupils of different abilities and learning styles to achieve. Assessment for Learning (AfL) opportunities should also be planned for this phase of the lesson. This is also the phase of the lesson where full teacher monitoring of pupils' learning should take place.

3. Conclusion

The concluding phase of the lesson requires you to consolidate the learning that has just taken place. This could be done through a question/answer session, through class discussion and/or through quizzes and games. Your job as a teacher is to reframe the responses given to you by the pupils, and then summarize the learning that has occurred during the lesson. Although good teachers will constantly monitor and assess pupil learning *as they teach*, rather than wait until the end of the lesson, most of you will not yet have the skills to do so fully. This makes your plenary session even more important. Your plenary session needs to be designed to assess the degree to which your learning objectives and outcomes have been realized. The final part of the lesson should see you linking the learning that has just occurred to the content of the next lesson.

What needs to be in your lesson plan?

Contextual information

This part of the plan should give information that provides a background to the lesson and sets the boundaries or limits of the plan. As an experienced observer I would expect you to include the following contextual information in your lesson plan:

- ☑ the name of the subject, unit of work and topic being studied;
- ☑ the date, time and place of the lesson;
- ☑ a seating plan;
- ☑ the gender and ethnic breakdown of the class;
- ☑ an explanation to show how a member of the support staff is being used and details of any SEN, EAL and/or G&T pupils;
- ☑ details of any pupils with social or behavioural problems;
- ☑ a description of your relationships with the pupils in the class;
- ☑ a description of the resources you intend to use;
- ☑ a description of how this lesson fits into the learning sequence. (What was learnt previously and how will this new learning feed into future lessons?)
- ☑ the attainment levels you are aiming to cater for. (You need to use National Curriculum, examination board or departmental assessment levels here.)
- ☑ the prior attainment data for each of the pupils;
- ☑ an indication of the assessment opportunities provided.

> If you are being observed by someone who doesn't know the class it is always advisable to provide them with a context document.

Learning objectives and outcomes

All lessons need *learning objectives*. You need to make it transparent as to what you expect pupils to know and understand by the end of the lesson. It is very common to confuse the tasks/activities that will be done in the lesson with learning objectives, so be wary of doing this. Schools will use different systems for setting objectives, but it is expected that pupils will know – by being told or by seeing these displayed on the board – what the learning objectives are. I would strongly advise that pupils copy down these learning objectives, or stick them into their books so that they can refer to them both during and after the lesson. When setting your learning objectives you need to be clear about what you expect the learning outcomes to be. Having said this, it will have already become pretty evident to you that not all pupils will be able to access the knowledge/skills/understanding you are trying to impart in your lessons to the same level, and because of this your outcomes need to be differentiated.

> In the true spirit of 'inclusion' it is vital that the work in your lessons is fully differentiated.

So what is actually meant by the term '**differentiation**'? 'It simply means teaching people differently according to their needs, their capabilities or even their preferred 'learning styles'. You need to make sure that you use a variety of teaching approaches capable of accommodating the different abilities and learning preferences of your pupils. Teachers who only group according to ability are limiting the learning of many pupils in their classes, particularly those with special educational needs. The best way to meet pupils' different learning needs is to deliver the curriculum in a number of different ways; to differentiate the vehicle by which the skills, knowledge and concepts are delivered, as well as by presenting a range of tasks designed to support learning. The reason for doing this is to ensure the maximum amount of pupil involvement, ie pupil planning, pupil assessment and pupil decision-making. In fact, the three can be fitted into a logical progression of teach, practise and assess. I have provided a number of types of differentiation:

- by classroom organization and grouping as a way of helping pupils to access knowledge, increase their understanding, develop concepts and practise skills;
- by paired tasks as a way of helping pupils to self-assess, peer assess, target-set and practise skills;
- by outcome as a way of both accessing knowledge and experiences and assessing at the end of the 'teach and practice' cycles;
- by resource in order to allow pupils to access information at their own level;
- by questioning in order to allow you to target your questions at specific pupils;
- by learning style and/or intelligence type in order to allow pupils to access information and/or present their work according to their preferred way of learning.

We all know from experience that pupils learn at different rates; some will have grasped the point before you have finished explaining it, and some may get there in the end but only after much additional effort and support. One way of formalizing the differentiation process is by posing the following three questions. By the end of this lesson, what should pupils know? What should pupils be able to understand? What should pupils be able to do? These may be expressed using the language of differentiation thus:

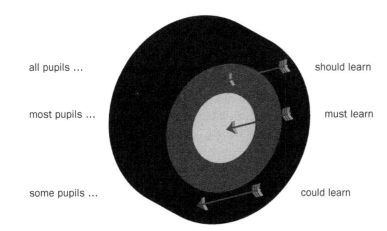

all pupils ...

most pupils ...

some pupils ...

should learn

must learn

could learn

An alternative but nevertheless effective way of differentiating outcomes is to use the 'must/should/could' formula, which really needs no further elaboration!

Whichever strategy you employ you need to use differentiated outcomes when drawing up schemes of work and lesson plans:

- so that even if pupils can only tackle *some* of the work, they will at least have covered the 'must learn' content;
- to make sure that more-able pupils who work at a faster pace have a constant supply of useful if not essential material to work on;
- to help check on any tendency on your part to stray from the learning objectives.

Starter activity

> The starter is an extremely important part of the lesson.

All lessons should have a starter activity. The purpose of the starter is to get pupils fully engaged in the learning process as soon as possible, and to engender a sense of pace within the lesson. Starter activities do not have to be directly linked to the main body of the lesson, although they are a good opportunity to use creative strategies to provide that all-important 'hook'. It is very important that your starter does not take too much time, and that it doesn't dominate the lesson. The starter activity could take on numerous forms, including:

- ☑ a brief quiz;
- ☑ a brief research task using reference book;
- ☑ an anagram or crossword puzzle;
- ☑ interpretation of visual or textual material;
- ☑ responding to questions having heard a music track, or having seen a brief video clip;
- ☑ paired discussion on a relevant topic;
- ☑ an opportunity to revisit and improve previous work.

Main activities

When selecting the activities and tasks you intend to use in your lesson, you need to think about a number of key questions:

> Divide the main section of your lesson into bite-size chunks and vary the activities to cater for the different learning styles of your pupils.

- Will the tasks and activities enable the learning objective(s) to be met?
- Will the tasks/activities enthuse and engage pupils of all ability levels? Will they enjoy learning?
- How successful will these tasks and activities be in catering for the different types of learners in your lesson?
- How can you use these tasks and activities to monitor and assess learning?

Plenary activity

Many beginning teachers find that because of their inability to plan effectively, this phase of the lesson often gets squeezed out. However, you do need to understand that this is a crucial part of the lesson because, if carried out properly, it will provide you and the pupils with an indication of whether the learning objectives have been met. As is the case with your starter activities, there is a range of possible formats for your plenary sessions. The suggestions made below, along with those made for starter activities, only 'scratch the surface' and you need to carry out more specific and focused research into this aspect of your teaching:

- ☑ verbal or written quizzes supported by a follow-up discussion;
- ☑ question/answer sessions in which you select responses from pupils across the ability range;
- ☑ role-play scenarios in which pupils are required to apply their newly gained knowledge, understanding and/or skills.

> Don't forget that plenary sessions do not just have to be planned for the end of the lesson.

Bearing in mind the vast range of subjects offered within primary and secondary schools today, it has been difficult to provide you with an exemplar lesson plan that is fully representative of all your needs. Subjects such as PE, science, technology and drama, for example, require planning strategies where health and safety issues play a major part of the planning process. In other subjects, health and safety plays a less dominant role. In presenting you with an exemplar lesson plan, I have included aspects of planning that may not be generally appropriate to your subject and or phase but which might, however, be needed for the occasional lesson.

Preparing your resources

> Be very careful to avoid 'death by worksheets'.

Having prepared your lesson plan, you will now have to think about preparing the resources to support your pupils' learning. The worksheet guidance shown below has been adapted from Butt (2006: 55) an excellent publication on lesson planning. Although the advice proffered below is extremely useful, you do need to be very careful to vary your resources and to not inflict 'death by worksheets' on your pupils.

Purpose

- What is the purpose of the worksheet?
- What are the learning objectives I want to cover?
- What specific subject knowledge, understanding and skills will the worksheet address (in the NC, GCSE or AS/A2 level)?

Planning

- What resources/materials do I need to construct the worksheet?
- Where are these available (textbooks, internet, CD-ROM, newspapers, photographs, cartoons, etc)? Are these resources up-to-date and free from bias?
- Do I have the technical ability to construct and reproduce the worksheets?
- What activities should be included to meet the 'purpose' outlined above? How will these activities be differentiated according to the abilities of the pupils?
- How will student learning be assessed?

Presentation

- What design do I want for the worksheet (portrait or landscape, font sizes and types, pictures, maps, cartoons, tables, diagrams, graphics, etc)? Will visual images reproduce clearly if the worksheet is to be photocopied?
- Is the text engaging and clearly sequenced for pupils? Is the text readable, and is the amount of technical vocabulary and use of jargon acceptable for the ability and age range of pupils being taught?
- What headings and labels do I need to include to signpost the activities to be undertaken? Is there too much/not enough text?
- Should key words (and their definitions) be identified in bold type?

Use

- To what degree does the worksheet support the lesson plan and its stated learning objectives?
- How will I introduce the worksheet to the pupils? Do I want them to complete it all in the lesson?
- Are any activities for homework? Are there different sheets and/or activities for different pupils?

Evaluation

- Did the worksheet help me achieve my learning objectives?
- Was the worksheet capable of providing differentiated learning for different abilities?
- Did the pupils find the worksheet interesting, motivating and stimulating to use?
- What might I change about the worksheet, or the way I used it, in future lessons?

Effective questioning

Questioning is one of the most extensively researched areas of teaching and learning. The purpose and rationale behind this research is to help us as educationalist to ascertain ways of conducting effective questioning sessions within our lessons. So, what exactly is meant by the term 'effective questioning'? Questioning is most effective when it allows pupils to become fully involved in, and engaged with, the learning process. While you are planning your lesson it is absolutely vital that you afford maximum thought to the types of questions you will be asking your pupils, and to the strategies you intend to use to create an 'inclusive' culture within the class. To this end you need be absolutely clear what the intended outcomes of your question/answer session should be.

> Plan your question/answer sessions in advance.

With this in mind I have provided you with a range of possible aims. A question/answer session could be designed to:

- ☑ interest, engage and challenge pupils;
- ☑ check on prior knowledge and understanding;
- ☑ stimulate recall, mobilizing existing knowledge and experience, to create new understanding and meaning;
- ☑ focus pupils' thinking on key concepts and issues;
- ☑ help pupils to extend their thinking from the concrete and factual to the analytical and evaluative;
- ☑ lead pupils through a planned sequence that progressively establishes key understanding;
- ☑ promote reasoning, problem solving, evaluation and the formulation of hypotheses; to promote pupils' thinking about the way they have learnt.

If you plan your question/answer session well enough, and in accordance with the principles of differentiation, you will undoubtedly cover a range of outcomes. However, it is fair to say that many teachers do not plan their question/answer sessions with any real rigour, and tend to think up their questions as they go along. I have carried out hundreds of lesson observations over the past 20 years and have been able to identify a number of pitfalls in the questioning styles used by many of these teachers. I have outlined these below.

Quality not quantity

Many teachers simply ask too many questions at once: exploring complex issues often requires us to ask complex questions. Since these questions are oral rather than written, pupils often find it difficult to understand what is required and soon become confused. When you are dealing with a complex subject, you need to tease out the issues for yourself first, and then focus your questions, introducing one line of enquiry at a time. The process is made more effective if we use direct concrete language and as few words as possible.

Scaffold your questioning

There is a tendency of many teachers to ask difficult questions without building up to these in a gradated manner. Sequencing questions in order of 'difficulty' is necessary to help pupils move to the higher levels of thinking.

Plan your questions in advance

Although some teachers ask a substantial number of questions in their lessons, many of these are superficial. As a result, pupils are not given the opportunity to get to the 'core' of an issue. You can avoid this problem by planning probing questions in advance. These can be built in as 'follow-up' questions designed to extend pupils' answers.

Understand why you are asking questions

Disappointingly, my observational evidence has demonstrated to me that many teachers are not always clear about exactly *why* they are asking questions: You will need to reflect on the kind of lesson you are planning before you think about the questions you intend to ask. Is it a lesson where you intend to focus mainly on facts, rules and/or sequences of actions? If this is the case, you will be more likely to ask closed questions that merely relate to knowledge. Alternatively, is it a lesson where you mainly intend to focus on comprehension, concepts and abstractions? If this is the case, you will be more likely to use open questions that relate to analysis, synthesis and evaluation.

Ask open questions

Reduce the number of 'closed' questions you ask your pupils. Asking 'open questions' helps to develop their thinking skills.

A common fault amongst many teachers, particularly in the field of maths, science and ICT, is that of asking predominantly closed questions that seek brief 'right or wrong' responses from their pupils. Although there is certainly a place for this approach, it is important that you challenge your classes by asking open questions wherever possible; making sure that you plan these in advance. Another strategy you could use is to establish an optimum length of response by saying something like, 'I don't want an answer of less than 15 words.'

Setting up a climate for effective questioning

In addition to establishing a 'safe and secure' emotional climate that caters for the reptilian brains of your pupils, you need to provide them with a stimulating, challenging and enquiring physical environment. I have provided you with a number of ways in which do this; these can be seen below.

Use your classroom display to enhance your questioning
Make maximum use of the classroom display space to present a range of different types of questions (and answers). These could be linked to pictures and/or text or could take the form of riddles, dingbats, questions in the form of jokes, general knowledge quiz questions, questions relating to exam techniques, conundrums, questions linked to careers, questions linked to moral dilemmas, etc.

Encourage participation in your questioning sessions
Get the pupils to see the value of participating verbally in lessons. If you want to get every pupil to make a verbal contribution to question/answer sessions, then they must understand the rationale for doing so. Pupils need to understand that absorbing information from written or verbal stimuli, of synthesizing this material, of formulating hypotheses and organizing their thoughts into a coherent language form, is all part of the

learning process. If you let pupils 'off the hook' too easily they are less likely to commit information/concepts to memory, and will be unlikely to gain full ownership of the material covered within the lesson. The rationale and importance of verbal participation in lessons by pupils should be established by you in your initial meetings with your classes, and should be constantly reinforced throughout the academic year. My early realization that this process needs to be translated into 'pupil speak' prompted me to design the diagram (from Dixie, 2007: 74) which I have used when trying to encourage pupils in my classes to participate in class discussions and question/answer sessions. You may find it useful.

> It is absolutely vital to provide pupils with the rationale for participating in class discussions and question/ answer sessions.

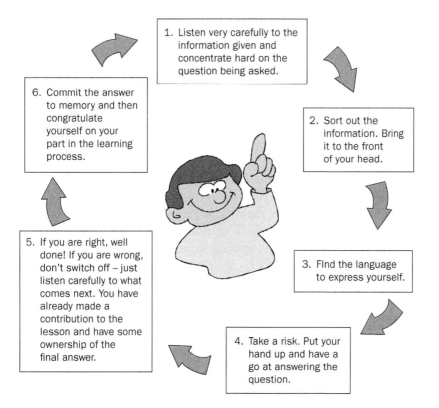

1. Listen very carefully to the information given and concentrate hard on the question being asked.

2. Sort out the information. Bring it to the front of your head.

3. Find the language to express yourself.

4. Take a risk. Put your hand up and have a go at answering the question.

5. If you are right, well done! If you are wrong, don't switch off – just listen carefully to what comes next. You have already made a contribution to the lesson and have some ownership of the final answer.

6. Commit the answer to memory and then congratulate yourself on your part in the learning process.

It is really important to ensure that every pupil makes a verbal contribution to lessons. For those really shy pupils who might find it excruciatingly embarrassing to put their hands up in class, you need to think about challenging them in an alternative manner. You could produce a set of cards with printed question mark signs on, and then ask your 'reluctant' pupils to move these cards surreptitiously to the front of the desk when they feel able to answer a question. Alternatively, you could get your pupils to use a shielded 'thumbs up' signal as a means of 'volunteering' responses in lessons. Where reluctant participants have contributed to question/answer sessions, it is important for you to ensure that their efforts are recognized. School credits, prize raffle tickets, postcards or phone calls home are just some of the ways in which you can do this.

The most successful question/answer sessions are those where the teacher has set up the parameters for behaviour beforehand.

Make sure that you **reinforce your expectations** and **rules** for each questioning session. Make it clear whether you want your pupils to put their hands up or whether you intend to select individuals to respond. Think about whether you want your pupils to answer questions individually or whether you want them to discuss these with their peers before offering a paired/group response. You may want to give pupils 'thinking' time before you seek responses from the class. All of these strategies are absolutely fine as long as it is you who determines the agenda. I have witnessed many scenarios where teachers, having insisted that pupils put their hands up, have then accepted responses from individuals who have 'shouted out' in class. Confusion arises when pupils are not clear about the rules of engagement. Failure to set up clear parameters for your questioning sessions will leave them in 'no-man's land' and unsure how to respond. Without good behaviour management, the development of effective questioning skills is unlikely to occur.

Make sure that you give pupils thinking time before you seek a response to your questions.

Make maximum use of **'wait time'**. The wait time concept has been a significant dimension in the research on teaching for a number of years. When teachers ask questions, they typically wait less than one second before asking a pupil to respond. Furthermore, after a pupil stops speaking, teachers generally react or respond with another question in less than one second. When teachers prolong their wait time between these exchanges to three seconds or longer, a number of effects are achieved, including:

- ☑ pupils give extended answers;
- ☑ pupils are likely to offer an answer of some kind;

☑ the number of 'I don't know' responses from pupils decreases;
☑ the responses that are given by pupils are more creative and thoughtful;
☑ the frequency of questions raised by pupils increases;
☑ the frequency of responses from less-able pupils increases;
☑ the number of hypothetical answers given by pupils increases significantly;
☑ teacher discipline moves decrease.

It is important to increase your range of questioning. Focusing on a small number of pupils and not involving the whole class is a common error. One way of avoiding this is to get the whole class to write their answers to closed questions and then show these to you en masse; some teachers use small whiteboards for this. Another possibility, which is probably more effective for more open questions, is to use the 'no-hands' strategy, where you pick the respondent rather than asking pupils to 'volunteer'. One advantage of this is that you can ask pupils questions of appropriate levels of difficulty. This is a good way of differentiating and goes a long way to ensuring inclusion.

Dealing ineffectively with wrong answers or misconceptions is also a common teaching error. Teachers sometimes worry that by correcting pupils they risk damaging their self-esteem. Providing verbal and visual prompts can often help pupils to correct their mistakes. It is important that you correct errors sensitively or, better still, that you use other pupils to correct these.

Many teachers do not treat pupils' answers seriously enough: they often simply ignore answers that appear to be slightly 'off-beam'. They can also fail to see the implications of these answers for pupil learning and miss opportunities to build upon these contributions. In situations such as these, you could ask pupils why they have offered these particular responses and/or if there is anything they would like to add. You could also ask the other pupils in the class to have a go at extending the original answer. In short, it is important not to cut pupils off and move on too quickly if they have given a wrong answer.

It is important to make use of your pupils' **Reticular Activating Systems** – the RAS is the part of the limbic brain that seeks relevance and asks 'what's in it for me'? In order to involve all of your pupils in the question/answer session, preface your questions with their individual names, and/or refer to individual pupils' contributions during a question/answer or discussion session. You could say something along the lines of: *'Paul made a really interesting comment earlier on and this fits in nicely with the work we are now doing.'* Doing this will provide Paul with a degree of status and will show him that you value his contribution. The net result of this is that he is more likely to behave appropriately and to remain involved in the lesson.

Tried and tested questioning strategies

Provide visual stimuli to support your question/answer sessions

Use photographs, drawings, prints and video clips as the bases for 'entry' or 'starter' tasks. Make use of animated clipart as visual clues for some of your questions; for example, if you were attempting to get the pupils to show their understanding of the term 'urbanization' you could start by displaying walking cartoon figures. Hopefully the pupils would be able to deduce from this image that urbanization involves the movement of people. The next animation you could display would be of a city with factories belching out smoke. With a little teasing you would be able to get the pupils to understand that urbanization involves people moving to urban areas to work in factories. At this point you could display the definition of urbanization in textual form. The point about this strategy is that pupils will have already arrived at the answer before any text has been displayed. There are numerous websites that sell some really useful animations and it is worth finding these on an internet search engine and your department subscribing to this service.

> Make use of visual images to support your questioning sessions.

Make your question/answer sessions kinaesthetic by using a value continuum

Ask pupils to move to a specific corner of the room according to whether they 'strongly agree', 'agree', 'disagree' or 'strongly disagree' about a particular issue. Allow and encourage pupils to move positions as new material is presented and/or when further questions are asked. Adopt the same technique using a linear continuum.

Use the 'mirroring' technique

When your pupils ask you a question, simply ask the same question back. For example, Pupil: *Why do some people eat so much?* Teacher: *Good question, why do you think some people eat so much?* Doing this encourages pupils' thinking skills and provides them with more ownership of the discussion.

Use the 'hot air balloon' technique

You need to get yourself a big sheet of paper and draw on it a hot air balloon tethered to the ground. On the balloon write the name of the project. eg 'Going Green', then pose the following five questions to the class:

1   Who needs to be on board? (Which people/things need to be on board for the idea to work?)
2   What needs to be right for the project to take off? (What human and material resources will be required?)
3   What is holding it back? (What social, economic, physical obstacles could stand in the way of the launch of this idea?)
4   What will really make it fly? (Things like enthusiasm, incentives, etc.)
5   What might blow the balloon off course? (What problems could cause the project to fail?)

Make full use of pupils' contributions in question/answer sessions

Use the 'bouncing' technique: *Josh ... What do you think of Rachel's idea?* '*Mary, how do you feel about what Josh has just said?*

> Vary your questioning strategies. Involve your pupils more in the process.

Use the 'think, pair and share' technique

Ask your pupils a question before pairing them up to discuss the issues. Having done this put the pupils into groups so that they can discuss the question further. When you are ready for pupils to give you their answers, seek group responses rather than responses from specific individuals. Many pupils feel safer making contributions when teachers use this questioning format.

Model the thinking process by 'thinking aloud' in front of your pupils

What am I going to say/write/do now? Why have I stopped? What is my problem? What sort of problem is this? Where have I seen this before? Who can help me? What do I need? What is the next step? Is there a better way? What alternatives are there?

Get pupils to 'think aloud' when they are preparing to offer their responses. Doing this raises the status of the 'thinking process' rather than just focusing pupils' attention on their final answer.

Provide questions designed to explore pupils' attitudes towards social and moral issues

Present pupils with moral dilemmas and produce a menu of questions to support the activity. For example, if you had been an adult in Hitler's Germany would you have joined the Nazi Party? Be prepared to justify your answer.

Provide pupils with opportunities to ask questions

> Get your pupils to ask questions. This provides ownership of the topic under study and increases motivation to learn.

On occasions, allow pupils to determine the direction of a lesson by the questions that they ask. For example, display a photograph or show a video clip of the topic under study and get pupils to ask what they want to know about this issue. Plan a section of the lesson given over entirely to pupils *asking* questions.

Use the 'hot-seating' method

Hot-seating is where a pupil adopts the role of a character from a book or a play, from a period in history, from another country, etc, and where he or she is put under a spotlight and asked questions by the audience. Because he or she is required to 'stay in character', even the most reserved pupil will find this process more comfortable than you might expect.

Planning your questions using Bloom's Taxonomy

Research (Wragg and Brown, 2001) suggests that lessons where questioning is most effective are likely to have a number of specific characteristics. These are as follows:

- where questions have been planned, visually displayed and closely linked to the objectives of the lesson;
- where the learning of basic skills has been enhanced by frequent questioning following the exposition of new content that has been broken down into bite-size pieces;
- where each step has been followed by guided practice that provides opportunities for pupils to consolidate what they have learnt and which allows teachers to check understanding;
- where closed questions have been used to check factual understanding and recall;
- where open questions have predominated in lessons;
- where sequences of questions have been planned so that cognitive levels increase as the questioning continues. This ensures that pupils have been encouraged to answer questions that demand increasingly higher-order thinking skills;
- where the classroom climate has been such that pupils have felt secure enough to take risks, be tentative and make mistakes.

In 1956, having researched thousands of questions routinely asked by teachers, Benjamin Bloom set about putting these into six categories. These categories came to be known as Bloom's Taxonomy. In the same year a committee of colleges led by Bloom carried out further work on this classification issue and identified three domains of educational activities. These are:

1   Cognitive: mental skills (Knowledge).
2   Psychomotor: manual or physical skills (Skills).
3   Affective: growth in feelings or emotional areas (Attitude).

The term 'domains' in an educational sense simply means 'categories'. Trainers often refer to these three domains as KSA (Knowledge, Skills, and Attitude). This taxonomy of learning behaviours can be thought of as 'the goals of the training process'; in other words once the learning session has finished, the learner should have acquired new skills, knowledge, and/or attitudes.

This compilation subdivides the three domains, starting from the simplest behaviour to the most complex. The divisions outlined are not absolutes and there are other systems or hierarchies that have been devised in the educational and training world. However, Bloom's Taxonomy is easily understood and is probably the most widely applied system today. For the purposes of this book, and without wishing to demote the significance of the other two domains, I am asking you to focus your attention primarily on the cognitive domain. Having said this, there is a real need for teachers to explore the other two domains in their lessons wherever possible.

Cognitive domain

The cognitive domain, shown on pp. 65–68, involves the development of knowledge and intellectual skills. This includes the recall or recognition of specific facts, procedural patterns and concepts that serve in the development of intellectual abilities and skills. There are six major categories, which are listed in order below, starting from the simplest behaviour to the most complex. The categories have been arranged as a hierarchy: in other words, the first one must be mastered before the next one can take place.

So, what exactly are the implications of Bloom's Taxonomy for your teaching and learning? The fundamental purpose of the taxonomy is to help you to plan a range of questions to support and challenge pupils of all abilities in your lessons. The emphasis here is on the word 'plan'. Your questions should not be 'hit and miss' but should be directed at those pupils to whom they are most appropriate; in short, you need to differentiate your questioning. To help you to do this I have presented further guidance below:

> Display a diagram showing Bloom's Taxonomy.

- Make this taxonomy clear to your pupils. Explaining the principles and purpose of Bloom's Taxonomy to your pupils, and presenting this to them in visual form in your classroom, is one way to get the pupils to understand why you will be asking different types of questions during your lessons. Bearing in mind the importance of getting pupils to ask questions, you could always provide the class with a visual stimulus (photograph, video clip, cartoon, print, etc) and ask your pupils to use

Bloom's Taxonomy to come up with a series of questions they would like to ask. Doing this will most certainly develop their questioning and thinking skills.

- When launching your learning objectives, produce a series of **key questions** that cover the range of categories found in Bloom's Taxonomy. You can use these questions to explore the level of pupils' understanding of the topic under study.

- The other thing you could do is to introduce a competitive element into your lessons by giving your questions a currency using Bloom's Taxonomy as a general guide. Your 'Knowledge' questions could be worth one point, your 'Comprehension' questions worth two points and so on. Pupils could amass points according to the types of questions they answer.

- Using Bloom's Taxonomy you could produce a series of colour-coded questions (each category being given a different colour) on one aspect of a unit of work you are teaching. You could ask your lower-ability pupils to choose one question from the first three categories (Knowledge, Comprehension, Application) and if they can manage it, one from another category. You could then get your more able pupils to select one or two questions from the more challenging categories. Doing this will involve pupils of all ability in the learning.

> You could differentiate your questions by using colour-coding and linking these to the various categories in Bloom's Taxonomy.

Bloom's Taxonomy

Knowledge

Useful Verbs	Sample Question Stems	Potential activities and products
Tell	What happened after...?	Make a list of the main events..
List	How many...?	Make a timeline of events.
Describe	Who was it that...?	Make a facts chart.
Relate	Can you name the...?	Write a list of any pieces of
Locate	Describe what happened at...?	information you can remember.
Write	Who spoke to...?	List all the .... in the story.
Find	Can you tell why...?	Make a chart showing...
State	Find the meaning of...?	Make an acrostic.
Name	What is...?	Recite a poem.
	Which is true or false...?	

Comprehension

Useful Verbs	Sample Question Stems	Potential activities and products
Explain Interpret Outline Discuss Distinguish Predict Restate Translate Compare Describe	Can you write in your own words...? Can you write a brief outline...? What do you think could have happened next...? Who do you think...? What was the main idea...? Who was the key character...? Can you distinguish between...? What differences exist between...? Can you provide an example of what you mean...? Can you provide a definition for...?	Cut out or draw pictures to show a particular event. Illustrate what you think the main idea was. Make a cartoon strip showing the sequence of events. Write and perform a play based on the story. Retell the story in your words. Paint a picture of some aspect you like. Write a summary report of an event. Prepare a flow chart to illustrate the sequence of events. Make a colouring book.

Application

Useful Verbs	Sample Question Stems	Potential activities and products
Solve Show Use Illustrate Construct Complete Examine Classify	Do you know another instance where...? Could this have happened in...? Can you group by characteristics such as...? What factors would you change if...? Can you apply the method used to some experience of your own...? What questions would you ask of...? From the information given, can you develop a set of instructions about...? Would this information be useful if you had a ...?	Construct a model to demonstrate how it will work. Make a diorama to illustrate an important event. Make a scrapbook about the areas of study. Make a paper-mache map to include relevant information about an event. Take a collection of photographs to demonstrate a particular point. Make up a puzzle game using the ideas from the study area. Make a clay model of an item in the material. Design a market strategy for your product using a known strategy as a model. Dress a doll in national costume. Paint a mural using the same materials. Write a textbook about... for others.

Analysis

Useful Verbs	Sample Question Stems	Potential activities and products
Analyse Distinguish Examine Compare Contrast Investigate Categorise Identify Explain Separate Advertise	Which events could have happened...? I ... happened, what might the ending have been? How was this similar to...? What was the underlying theme of...? What do you see as other possible outcomes? Why did ... changes occur? Can you compare your ... with that presented in...? Can you explain what must have happened when...? How is ... similar to ...? What are some of the problems of...? Can you distinguish between...? What were some of the motives behind...? What was the turning point in the game? What was the problem with...?	Design a questionnaire to gather information. Write a commercial to sell a new product. Conduct an investigation to produce information to support a view. Make a flow chart to show the critical stages. Construct a graph to illustrate selected information. Make a jigsaw puzzle. Make a family tree showing relationships. Put on a play about the study area. Write a biography of the study person. Prepare a report about the area of study. Arrange a party. Make all the arrangements and record the steps needed. Review a work of art in terms of form, colour and texture.

Synthesis

Useful Verbs	Sample Question Stems	Potential activities and products
Create Invent Compose Predict Plan Construct Design Imagine Propose Devise Formulate	Can you design a ... to ...? Why not compose a song about...? Can you see a possible solution to...? If you had access to all resources how would you deal with...? Why don't you devise your own way to deal with...? What would happen if...? How many ways can you...? Can you create new and unusual uses for...? Can you write a new recipe for a tasty dish? can you develop a proposal which would...	Invent a machine to do a specific task. Design a building to house your study. Create a new product. Give it a name and plan a marketing campaign. Write about your feelings in relation to... Write a TV show, play, puppet show, role play, song or pantomime about...? Design a record, book, or magazine cover for...? Make up a new language code and write material using it. Sell an idea. Devise a way to... Compose a rhythm or put new words to a known melody.

Evaluation

Useful Verbs	Sample Question Stems	Potential activities and products
Judge Select Choose Decide Justify Debate Verify Argue Recommend Assess Discuss Rate Prioritise Determine	Is there a better solution to... Judge the value of... Can you defend your position about...? Do you think ... is a good or a bad thing? How would you have handled...? What changes to ... would you recommend? Do you believe? Are you a ... person? How would you feel if...? How effective are...? What do you think about...?	Prepare a list of criteria to judge a ... show. Indicate priority and ratings. Conduct a debate about an issue of special interest. Make a booklet about 5 rules you see as important. Convince others. Form a panel to discuss views, e.g. "Learning at School." Write a letter to ... advising on changes needed at... Write a half yearly report. Prepare a case to present your view about...

From Dalton, J. and Smith, D. (1986) 'Extending Children's Special Abilities – Strategies for primary classrooms' Victoria Ministry for Education pp 36–7.

Emergency planning

Let's face it – even if you are the best practitioner in the school, things do go wrong occasionally. How many times have you been all set to deliver an 'all singing, all dancing' lesson only to discover that the school's ICT system has gone down? What about the times when you have planned a lesson expecting the whole class to be present, only to find out late in the day that many of the pupils are out of school on an unpublicized school trip? How many times have personal and/or professional crises led to you being unable to prepare your lesson thoroughly? My advice to you is to produce a bank of emergency 'back-up' lessons and resources on topic areas taken from your scheme of work or syllabus. These could be stored in a central filing cabinet in the department office or separately in your own classroom. 'Oh no, not more work!' I hear you say. This will not necessarily be the case. By exchanging a few lesson plans and resources with other colleagues in your department, you will already have amassed a significant bank of emergency lesson material. Of course, it really does help if the department has a common and agreed lesson planning format, as this will help to make the learning objectives and learning journey absolutely transparent. In addition to using your colleagues to support this process, you can download free lesson plans from the internet. Here are some useful sites:

Promethean Planet: www.prometheanplanet.com
Chalkface: www.chalkface.com
About.Com: www.about.com
Hotchalk lesson plans page: www.lessonplanspage.com
Schoolzone: www.schoolzone.co.uk
Teachernet: www.teachernet.com

Having provided you with this information, I feel it important to stress that you are advised to use these resources frugally. There is simply no substitute for producing lesson plans that fully take the individualized needs of the pupils in your classes into consideration.

> Prepare for the 'unexpected' – it's bound to happen.

Evaluating your lessons

To a greater or lesser degree, all teachers are expected to evaluate their lessons and to reflect upon the ways in which they can improve their practice. If you are a teacher trainee, you may find that your training provider has furnished you with a set of 'evaluative' questions to be answered. If you are an NQT or person in your early years of teaching, you may want to continue with this format. Alternatively, you may be in a school where you will be left entirely to your own devices. If this is the case, I would strongly suggest that you read the following text about the nature and value of **reflective practice** and you make full use the reflective formula provided for you below.

> An understanding of the reflective process is a crucial development tool.

I firmly believe that reflective practice, introduced by Donald Schön in his book *The Reflective Practitioner* (1983), lies at the very heart of the teaching profession. Schön describes reflective practice as being the process of thoughtfully considering one's own experiences in applying knowledge to practice while being coached by professionals in the discipline. In education, it refers to the process of the teacher studying his or her own teaching methods and determining what works best for the pupils. For the purposes of this book I am going to use the work of Schön to help you to briefly explore the issue of reflective practice. My rationale for focusing on Schön's work is that his ideas have been extremely influential in initial teacher training in Britain in recent years.

Schön (1983) cited in Furlong and Maynard (1995), emphasizes that teachers have to cope with the fact that no two groups of pupils are alike and that even with pupils with whom they are familiar, they are constantly having to face new scenarios and present new material to them. This inevitably creates its own unique problems in terms of explanation and understanding. The teacher has to constantly react to the ever-changing scenarios that occur in his or her classroom in such a way that the process appears to be seamless to the pupils. My experience tells me that many pupils are very perceptive in being able to identify lack of fluidity in lessons and that if they perceive there to be 'gaps' in the flow of the lesson, they are extremely skilled in filling those gaps with inappropriate behaviour.

Schön called the process of constantly reacting to ever-changing scenarios 'reflection-*in*-action'. Reflection-*in*-action occurs when a practitioner faces an unknown situation. In these circumstances, the practitioner is able to bring certain aspects of his or her work to his or her level of consciousness, reflect upon it and reshape it without interrupting the flow of proceedings. It is fair to say that as you become more experienced you will tend to do this quite naturally and intuitively, without thinking too deeply about the process. However, beginning teachers tend to struggle with this process and they often become somewhat flustered when new scenarios are presented to them. It is important for you to know that some of the unpredictable and untoward things that are highly likely to throw you 'off track' in the initial stages of your teaching will be of little or no consequence as you become more experienced.

As you become more experienced you will develop the skill of 'reflection-*in*-action', which is the ability to evaluate and modify your practice as it happens.

Reflection-*in*-action therefore largely involves 'situated knowledge' and is a process that we often go through without necessarily being able to say exactly what we are doing. Reflecting on and articulating our thoughts about our teaching *after* the lesson has happened is called '**reflection-*on*-action**' and it is also something that many teachers find challenging. Even some of the very best teachers often find it difficult to articulate all the things they do intuitively in the classroom to produce a good lesson. I fully agree with Schön that reflection-*on*-action is a key process in learning how to teach. In Schön (1983) he argues that no matter how inadequate a beginning teacher's verbal reconstruction of events, it is only by constantly bringing the ways in which they are framing their teaching situations to their level of consciousness that they will eventually gain control of their own teaching. This quote from Schön (1987) cited in Furlong and Maynard (1995), makes the point clearly:

Most beginning teachers are more comfortable in 'reflecting-*on*-action', which requires them to evaluate their practice after the event.

> As I think back on my experience ... I may consolidate my understanding of the problem or invent a better or more general solution to it. If I do, my present reflection on my earlier reflection-in-action begins a dialogue of thinking and doing through which I become more skilful.

So how does this process work in practice? The first thing you need to do is simply to *describe* the professional scenario presented to you. This could be something that happened in the classroom, an incident in the school corridor, or your observations of interactions between colleagues and/or pupils. At this point in the reflective process there is no evaluative input whatsoever – you merely need to describe the scenario.

Having done this, you now need to describe the perceived consequences of what you have just experienced; in other words, what happened because of what happened. For example, you may have noticed that in one of your lesson observations that a music teacher failed to establish his or her expectations, rules and sanctions before allowing the pupils to carry out an experiment. The consequences of him or her not doing this might have been that the pupils behaved in an unruly fashion thus disrupting learning in the lesson. Another consequence could be that some of the music equipment was damaged as a result of horseplay in the rehearsal room. I call these crucial decision-making factors in a lesson 'watershed moments' because they represent specific points in lessons where teachers' actions or inactions can lead to varying and sometimes adverse consequences (Dixie, 2007). When I was a professional tutor in a large comprehensive school I asked my trainees to carry out lesson observations that require them to identify these watershed moments in lessons, and to then describe the consequences arising from these. You will also note from Figure 5.2 that this is also the place to describe your emotional responses to the scenarios presented to you. In two of my books (Dixie, 2005; 2007) I give a high profile to the importance of exploring the emotional side of teaching. I feel strongly that recognizing and dealing with your emotional responses to teaching is an important part of the reflective process.

Reflection without action is a hollow process. It is important to show some tangible results of the reflective process.

Experience shows me that most beginning teachers are very skilled at describing professional scenarios but are far less adept at recognizing watershed moments and/or their potential consequences. Unless advised to the contrary this is where their reflective practice usually ends. They neither identify the implications of their teaching experiences nor do they show how they have modified or altered their practice in the light of their reflections. If the reflective cycle illustrated in Figure 5.2 is to be successfully realized then the third and fourth requirements need to be realized. Having responded to your reflections by taking the appropriate action, the whole reflective process starts over again. This document does not have to be completed electronically or in the column form presented here. It is, however, very important that the criteria in all four stages are met if you want to demonstrate your skill as a reflective practitioner and if you want to provide evidence of having moved your practice on.

Identification/ description of professional scenarios.	What are the perceived consequences of these behaviours?	What are the implications and targets for your professional practice?	What evidence can you provide to show how you have used this experience to develop your practice and to inform your behaviour in professional scenarios?
▪ Lesson observation	▪ Identify teaching and learning consequences by looking for 'watershed' moments.	▪ How will you use this information to inform your professional practice?	How do you know whether you have been successful?
▪ Out of classroom scenarios			
▪ Interaction with colleague(s)	▪ Identify the emotional consequences for you as a teacher. Did the incident make you feel proud, angry, disappointed, disempowered etc?	▪ What targets will you set yourself?	E.g. Planning lessons with pupils' learning styles in mind.
▪ Interaction with parents/ carers		▪ What strategies will you use?	E.g. Dealing with a challenging situation in a non-confrontational manner.
In other words simply describe what happened.		▪ How are you going to use these emotions to inform your future practice?	E.g. Being proactive in seeking advice and guidance from colleagues.

E.g. Evidence of using knowledge of pupils' background to inform planning. |

Figure 5.2 Reflective Formula

Table 5.1 Exemplar extract from Reflective Journal

Identification/ Description of professional scenarios.	What are the perceived consequences of these behaviours?	What are the implications and targets for your professional practice?	What evidence do you have to show how you have used this experience to develop your professional practice?
This week I have conducted a pupil trail with the purpose of observing a variety of teachers in a variety of settings and subjects. The focus of these observations was effective classroom management and effective pupil learning.	Having made observations I listed common points for good classroom management. These points generally revolved around good preparation and resources. I was surprised that many classes were clear on the expectations of them as they entered the room. This is because the rules and consequences were established early on, and frequently returned to. In the cases where the behaviour policy is referred to, successful management was only apparent in cases where threats were followed up. Praise and positive attitudes from teachers were also apparent in lessons with good pace, character, behaviour and learning.	I will ensure that when I begin teaching next week I will establish my rules, rewards and consequences in line with the schools behaviour policy at the beginning of the lesson. I will do this with each of the classes and ensure the pupils are clear about their responsibilities in keeping with these. I will supply each student with a copy of the expectations in class and ask them to sign in agreement and stick the rules to their booklets for future reference.	Having taken over four classes already, I have introduced my expectations as mentioned. I have clearly displayed laminates at the front of the room and the pupils have agreed and kept a copy glued to their books.

Instead of just arriving and imposing my rules on the class, I have begun each new group's lesson with a Q&A discussion, asking the pupils to suggest appropriate rules they feel all should abide to in my room. I noted these on the board and reflected the similarities between these and the rules I have established. I found this discussion enforced their responsibility as they suggested the majority of them. |

From 'The Trainee Primary Teacher's Handbook Page 122 Gererd Dixie and Janet Ball 2009 Continuum

6 Getting your subject knowledge up to date

Developing your subject knowledge for teaching

My many conversations with beginning teachers demonstrate to me that one of their biggest areas of concern is their perceived vulnerability as far as their level of subject knowledge is concerned. This is particularly the case for trainees who qualified with joint degrees and/or for those who have been away from the world of academia for some time. It is also the case for those teachers who have been asked to teach a subject they have not been trained in. This happens a lot in secondary schools when senior members of staff responsible for producing the timetable discover a mismatch between the number of lessons needing to be taught and the number of specialized staff available to teach them.

The fundamental question often asked by these teachers is: is my subject knowledge good enough to effectively support the learning of my pupils? What many of these teachers do not fully take on board is that knowledge of subject matter alone is not sufficient. You need to know how to deliver this knowledge in an accessible manner to your pupils; hence your need to also gain a secure knowledge of relevant pedagogy. Subject knowledge and understanding cover a range of elements:

- teaching, learning and behaviour management strategies;
- assessment;
- subject knowledge for teaching;
- understanding the relevant statutory and non-statutory curricula;
- use of literacy, numeracy and ICT to support your teaching and wider professional activities.

75

Having a secure subject knowledge can impact positively on your behaviour management.

As beginning teachers, you will need to prove that you have a sufficiently secure grasp of the concepts, ideas and principles relevant to your subject. You can show this secure subject and pedagogical knowledge by demonstrating your ability to:

- ☑ plan individual lessons in an effective and challenging manner;
- ☑ plan effective and challenging sequences of lessons and schemes of work;
- ☑ set challenging teaching and learning objectives;
- ☑ assess pupils' progress towards these objectives;
- ☑ set subject-related targets for individuals and groups of pupils;
- ☑ react confidently and accurately to pupils' questions;
- ☑ successfully break down ideas and concepts and sequence them logically to support the development of pupils' knowledge and understanding;
- ☑ recognize and respond to pupils' common misconceptions;
- ☑ make effective interventions to construct and scaffold pupils' learning;
- ☑ analyse pupils' progress and make accurate assessments of their learning and achievement;
- ☑ hold informed discussions with your tutors and colleagues;
- ☑ produce effective essays and/or assignments on related issues.

With the exception of those of you who are only teaching Key Stage 5 pupils, you will need to demonstrate a knowledge and understanding of the relevant aspects of the National Curriculum, as set out in the *National Curriculum Handbook*. You will need to demonstrate that you fully understand the three principles of inclusion: the need to set suitable learning challenges; the need to respond to pupils' diverse needs; and the need to find ways to overcome barriers to learning and assessment for individuals and groups. You will need to reflect your understanding of these principles in your lesson planning and teaching. You are also required to know about, and understand, the principles and approaches to teaching underpinning the National Strategy relevant to the age range you are teaching. If relevant to your subject, you will be expected to have a knowledge and understanding of the National Curriculum programmes of study. You will also be expected to have and demonstrate a secure knowledge of the examination syllabus of the subject(s) you are teaching. If you are teaching a vocational subject in the 14–19 phase, you will need to demonstrate a secure knowledge and understanding of your subject and show that you are familiar with the Secondary National Strategy.

> You need to know and understand the relevant statutory and non-statutory curricula frameworks.

Although you may not actually teach PSHE, if you are a teacher trainee you will nevertheless be expected to demonstrate your familiarity with the National Curriculum guidance on this subject relevant to the age ranges you are training to teach. If you are a secondary school teacher you need to be aware that the 14–19 Curriculum is subject to continuous change and you are expected to keep up to date with these developments. You can show your competence in this area by demonstrating your ability to:

> You need to be aware of the potential impact of the 14–19 Curriculum.

- ☑ make reference to the relevant curricula, frameworks and initiatives in your planning;
- ☑ plan for and practise inclusion in your lessons;
- ☑ show your knowledge and understanding of National Strategy approaches in your planning and teaching;
- ☑ hold informed discussions with your mentors and/or colleagues;
- ☑ produce effective essays and/or assignments on related issues.

If you are a teacher trainee, the TDA (Training and Development Agency), through the medium of the training providers, will require you to identify your subject and pedagogical knowledge throughout your training year. Although you will have entered the profession at degree level, it would be totally unfair and unrealistic to expect you to hold sufficient subject and pedagogical knowledge to be able to confidently teach a range of topics to pupils across the age ranges you are being trained to teach. It is with this in mind that training providers have been asked to audit your subject/pedagogical knowledge at the beginning of the course, and to monitor your progress in this field throughout your training year. It is up to you, therefore, to make sure that you provide evidence to illustrate this progress. Should you require further details of exactly how to monitor and record your subject knowledge development then I suggest you refer to *The Trainee Secondary Teacher's Handbook* (Dixie, 2009a) which provides numerous examples of how to do this.

Section 2

Reading and responding to the signs

In just the same way that you need to modify your driving behaviour when encountering instructional road signs while on a car journey, you need to adapt your teaching practice in accordance with the instruction and guidance proffered to you by your mentors and trainers. The aims of this section are threefold. Continuing with the analogy of teaching as a journey and using a range of road signs as visual prompts, this section will endeavour to: a) explore how the command sign could be deemed relevant to a teacher's professional scenario, b) provide advice and guidance as to how to employ relevant strategies, and c) provide exemplars of good practice.

7 Avoiding conflict

Picture this scenario. Aaron, a particularly challenging Year 6 pupil has done his very best to scupper your lesson plans by constantly shouting out, talking to his peers and making stupid noises in class. Despite countless requests from you for him to stop, he continues to behave in a totally inappropriate manner. At the point where you have simply had enough, you ask him to leave the classroom and to stand out in the corridor until you can find the time to talk to him. He refuses point blank to move. You raise the tenor of your voice, accompany this with the most assertive body language you can muster, and repeat your instruction for him to leave the classroom. He still refuses to move. Now you begin to realize that you have a serious issue. You feel that if you back down you will lose your status and credibility with the rest of the pupils in the class. Aaron, however, feels exactly the same and is worried about the possibility of losing face in front of his peers. As a result of this, an impasse is reached.

> Prepare yourself for the inevitable impasse. Have a strategy in place to deal with this.

So, what usually happens next in situations such as these? Unfortunately in rather too many cases, pupils like Aaron tend to 'win the day'. The teacher backs down by half-heartedly saying something along the lines of, 'Well, if you won't move, then you'd just better behave yourself for the rest of the lesson.' In this scenario the teacher leaves the lesson feeling totally disempowered. Aaron, on the other hand, leaves the lesson feeling on top of the world, fully cognisant of the fact that it is he, and not the teacher, who is 'running the agenda'. An alternative, but only marginally more effective strategy adopted by many teachers in situations such as these is to seek the support of their colleagues, usually a member of the senior management team. I need to stress that there is nothing intrinsically wrong with using your colleagues to help you out at times like these, but this tactic must be used sparingly. (I offer strategies to help you to do this effectively in Section 3.) However, the notable outcome of these two scenarios is that in both cases the teacher leaves the lesson feeling disempowered.

So how can you create a situation where, although a pupil refuses to carry out your instructions, you still manage to remain fully in control and empowered? The answers to this question are twofold. First, you need to think very carefully about the type of language you use to address the intransigent pupil; second, you need to ensure that you have the tenacity and energy to follow up on the incident.

> Be prepared to 'tactically withdraw' when necessary.

The first thing to remember in scenarios such as these is that you may need to stop and give way and tactically withdraw until you can deal with the situation more effectively. As long as you accompany this temporary withdrawal with appropriate and assertive language that will empower you, you will be able to give yourself a dignified way out of the situation. I have provided guidance on how to do this below.

Adopt a neutral and rather 'matter of fact' stance in your body language and tone of voice, and say something along the lines of:

> *Aaron, I have asked you to leave the classroom and you have refused to do so. I cannot physically make you move but you, and the rest of the class, need to know that I will most certainly follow up on this incident as soon as the lesson ends and that there will be serious consequences. However, if you decide to leave the room now, then the only person you will have to deal with will be me. The choice is yours.*

If Aaron decides to leave the room at this point, inwardly breathe a sigh of relief and give him five minutes or so 'calming down' time before going out into the corridor to talk to him. Although it is imperative that some form of sanction is issued, you do need to remember to keep your promise about not involving other members of staff in the process. However, if Aaron fails to comply with your instructions, tactically ignore him for the rest of the lesson and deal with the issue later. If there is a classroom nearby and you feel comfortable in doing so, then notify a colleague of your intentions and move the rest of the class into this room leaving Aaron on his own in your room.

The fundamental learning point about this type of incident is that you do not have to deal with conflict scenarios there and then. And this is where the second point comes in. In the event of a pupil disobeying your instructions, be prepared to **'stop'** and **'give way'** and to deal with the matter when you and the pupil have calmed down. Trying to break the impasse will only lead to a shouting match and will result in both you and the pupil not only losing your temper, but also your dignity. Having said this, it is absolutely vital that you do what you said you would do -- follow up this incident with senior colleagues and make the results of your actions known to the class next time you see them. It is important to remember that sanctions can be deferred. They do not have to be immediate. It is the **certainty not the severity** that counts.'

8 Achieving consistency in behaviour management

I have used these signs to illustrate the need for teachers to demonstrate **consistency** in their behaviour management and not to deviate from the behaviour management plans. Contemporary literature on the functions of the brain describes how the reptilian brain is primarily responsible for routine bodily functions such as breathing, heartbeat, blood pressure and balance. It is the primeval part of the brain that takes charge of our survival responses and helps us to judge whether we should 'take flight' or 'fight'. As is also the case in the animal world, the reptilian brain predisposes us to a system of social conformity, of being able to know one's place in the pecking order and of possessing the need to respond to ritualistic rules.

One of the hindrances to pupil learning is 'insecurity'. Setting out clear ground rules and expectations and being fair and consistent are essential in reducing insecurity among pupils. Despite the overt resistance of many youngsters to rules and routines, I am convinced that there is a large part of them that subconsciously demands these boundaries and this level of structure within their lessons. By providing your pupils with a system of well-defined rules, routines and sanctions you will be giving these youngsters the security they need at this crucial stage of their lives, and in doing so you will be providing a firm foundation for learning. Don't just take my word for it. One of the many psychologists who explored this issue

> The reptilian brain seeks security, safety and consistency. Adopting a consistent approach towards your behaviour management provides this.

was Abraham Maslow who is renowned for creating his **'hierarchy of human needs'**. Beyond the details of air, water, food and sex, he laid out five needs in the following order: the physiological, safety and security, love and belonging, esteem and self-actualization. These needs can be seen in Figure 8.1.

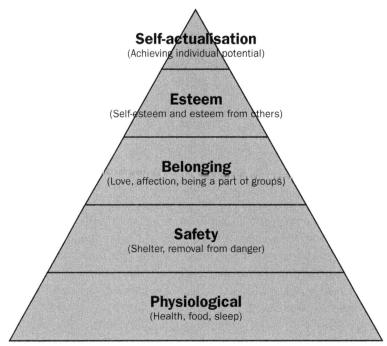

Reproduced with kind permission from 'Changing Minds', http://changingminds.org/explanations/needs/maslow.htm

Figure 8.1 Maslow's Hierarchy of Needs

Although I believe that teachers need to have a basic understanding of all human needs, for the purpose of this book I want you to focus your attention on the second set of needs in the hierarchy – 'safety needs'. When the physiological requirements have been catered for, this second layer of needs comes into play. In this stage, human beings become increasingly interested in finding safe circumstances, stability and protection. By doing so, they develop the need for structure, order and some degree of limit in their lives. In the classroom this manifests itself in the need for rules, routines and sanctions; in other words, well-defined boundaries designed to govern pupil behaviour. Carrying out these simple measures on a consistent basis will certainly help to prevent the irritating, low-level, disruptive behaviour that is detrimental to effective teaching and learning. It is worth spending time thinking about the sorts of rules and routines you will need to set up in your classes.

> Pupils need boundaries, so adopt a 'firm but fair' approach.

When carrying out research into 'what makes a good teacher' one of the main characteristics identified by pupils is that of 'firmness'. Pupils talk fondly of those teachers with whom they can 'have a laugh' but who nevertheless establish *and* maintain transparent rules, routines, rewards and sanctions and 'define boundaries' in their classes. To this end it is absolutely vital that you give your full attention to what Rogers (1998) calls the **'establishment phase'** and that you reinforce your behavioural expectations, sanctions and rewards on a consistent basis throughout the year.

When starting to think about the establishment phase it is important to remember that managing pupils' behaviour should never simply be done for its own sake, nor should the importance of establishing and maintaining good working relationships be ignored. Maintaining good discipline in lessons while at the same time showing how much you enjoy the company of young people is a tall order for the beginning teacher. The importance of getting the balance right can be seen in the following quote:

> *Taking a class is like playing a salmon – a slight change of direction here, a discreet tightening of the line there, and so on. If you are too insensitive, you will not only break the line but lose the fish as well.* (Source unknown)

You could be the most creative and imaginative teacher in the world and enjoy warm relationships with pupils, but if you do not establish a firm but fair behaviour management regime in your lessons

> Low-level disruption is easily eradicated by establishing your rules, routines, rewards and sanctions early on.

they will not learn. In a climate of confusion and ambiguity even the most motivated of pupils will soon begin to lose heart and a downward spiral of poor behaviour and performance will occur. My observations of colleagues at work in the classroom, along with my secondary research, indicate that this poor behaviour is very often low level and that it can be easily eradicated through a robust establishment phase.

Most poor behaviour in lessons is low-level and easily eradicated

So, what do you need to do to establish your high expectations of pupils' behaviour in your lessons? Before you start to think about your establishment phase you need to work extremely hard on your body language and tone of voice. You need to convey to the pupils that **'you say what you mean and mean what you say'.** Having said this I wouldn't advise taking this as far as this Moroccan Teacher did in 2003:

Pupils thrown out of window

Two Moroccan schoolboys were injured yesterday when their woman teacher threw them out of a first floor window for being too noisy. One, aged nine was taken to hospital in Casablanca with a broken shoulder and head injuries. The other, aged ten was only slightly hurt. An education official said the teacher had warned the pair she would throw them out. 'They did not listen. They should have,' he said.

Reuters, Rabat, 10 October 2003

Ok, so this is quite a humorous example but there is a serious aspect to this issue. Allow me to share the result of some low-level research carried out with my Year 11 classes just before I left teaching. I asked them to imagine that they were encountering a teacher for the very first time before then asking them these two questions:

- How long does it take you to make a judgement about whether you are going to behave for this teacher or not?
- On what factors do you base your decision?

You may be alarmed to note that the net response to first question given by the pupils in all three classes was between *five and ten minutes.* However, you probably will not be surprised when I tell you that the overriding factors that contribute to this decision are the body language and tone of voice of the teacher.

Although this was a low-level piece of research, my experience and subsequent discussions with teenagers indicates to me that you have an incredibly brief period of time in which to make a positive impression. The implications of this research are obvious. Irrespective of how lacking in confidence you may be, it is imperative that you adopt assertive body language and tone of voice to establish a culture of learning for the rest of your time with these pupils.

> **Pupils make their minds up about a teacher very quickly.**

Wragg (1995: 115) writes about the need for teachers to be skilled in the area of **'impression management'** and describes the process of impression management that commences on first meeting and continues through subsequent encounters:

> *The individual's initial projection commits him to what he is proposing to be and requires him to drop all pretences of being other things. As the interaction among the participants progresses, additions and modifications in this informational state will, of course, occur but it is essential that these later developments be related without contradiction to, and even built up from the initial positions taken up by several participants.*

In short, we should not give pupils 'mixed messages'. With the significance of 'impression management' firmly in your mind when you first meet your new classes you need to:

Be aware of your need to make an early impression with your pupils.

☑ Enter the room with a firm tread, holding your head high, with your chin tilted slightly forward and your shoulders back, maintaining a confident pose.

☑ Use an assertive, confident and decisive tone of voice, changing your pitch to stimulate interest in what you are saying. Research indicates that the more 'strident' the voice, the less effective it is as a behaviour management/teaching tool. If you have to raise your voice to gain attention then do so, but at the point when you have got the pupils' attention, lower your tone in graduated steps. Avoid constant hesitations such as 'er', 'um', etc. In short, ensure that you use what I call the 'language of inevitability' –make the assumption both in the content and the tone of your discourse that you expect pupils to carry out your instructions. This will not always be 100 per cent successful but will work most of the time.

☑ Stand in full view of the class so you can scan the room and make full eye contact with your pupils to make sure that they are focusing their attention on you.

☑ Avoid using exaggerated hand and body movement. (This tends to distract pupils' attention from what you are actually saying).

Formalize the learning process by producing a teacher/pupil contract.

In this establishment phase you need to stress that expectations are not 'one-way' and that pupils have a right to be taught and to receive feedback. To this end it is always worth using a PowerPoint slide or poster to get this 'contractual' point of view across. Examples of pupil/teacher and teacher/pupil contracts are shown in Boxes 8.1 and 8.2.

Having outlined the advantages of establishing a working partnership with your pupils, I need to make the point that it is *you* who should ultimately be the one in control of the learning/teaching scenarios. You could convey this message to the pupils by presenting them with the expectations and rules presented in the 'contracts'. It is important to note that if you take the time and trouble to provide the rationale behind these rules and expectations, you are more likely to experience success in their implementation. The contract templates (from Dixie, 2007: 17) are also available online on the companion website (http://education.dixie.continuumbooks.com).

> Providing pupils with the rationale behind your expectations and rules goes a long way to producing a positive learning environment.

PUPIL/TEACHER CONTRACT

WHAT DO I EXPECT FROM YOU?

- I expect you to be courteous to me and to the other pupils in the class.
- I expect your <u>full</u> attention when I ask for it. This will help you to learn.
- I expect you to be honest about yourself and to admit when you are in the wrong. (This is all part of the learning process)
- I expect you to meet assignment deadlines. (This helps me to help you)
- I expect you to do your very best. It is very important that you are able to look back at your efforts over the year with pride.
- I expect you to accept the following consequences of not doing the above.
  I will speak to you in private.
  If you persist then I will give you a detention
  I will contact your H.O.Y.
  I will contact your parents.

Box 8.1

TEACHER/PUPIL CONTRACT

WHAT CAN YOU EXPECT FROM ME?

- You can expect me to be courteous and respectful even when I am telling you off.
- You can expect my full efforts in helping you to progress and/or helping through your difficulties.
- You can expect me to mark your work on a regular basis and to provide you with constructive feedback.
- You can expect me to apologise to you or the class when I get things wrong.
- You can expect me to treat you fairly and consistently for misbehaviour or for poor work ethic.

Signed   Teacher .... **Pupil** ....

From *Managing Your Classroom*, Gererd Dixie (2007: 17)

Box 8.2

Provided you launch these expectations and rules in a robust and assertive manner, and provided that you reinforce these on a consistent basis, I see no reason why they shouldn't help prevent that irritating, low-level, disruptive behaviour which is so detrimental to effective teaching and learning. However, your work with the establishment phase doesn't end there. It is unrealistic to simply launch your general expectations, rules rewards and sanctions and expect pupils to apply these to a whole host of learning scenarios. It is worth spending time in thinking about the sorts of rules and routines that you will need to set up for *each* specific type of activity/task in your lessons. Below is a list of teaching/learning activities and scenarios that all require their own distinct set of behaviour codes. My question to you is – how robust are you in outlining your parameters/expectations and sanctions for each specific activity? Do your pupils know what you want them to do? Do they know how you want them to do it? Do they know what will happen if they disobey your instructions?

> Set up firm parameters for each and every activity.

If my observations are anything to go by, many teachers give very little thought to the launching phase of the tasks and activities planned for the lesson. To this end, I would like you to think about the expectations, rules, rewards and sanctions you might present to pupils in the following scenarios:

- when taking the register;
- when carrying out group or paired work;
- when running question/answer or discussion sessions;
- when carrying out formal testing of the pupils;
- when overseeing pupils' presentations;
- when pupils enter or leave a classroom;
- when pupils transition from one activity to another;
- when pupils are carrying out independent work;
- when pupils are clearing up;
- when you are giving a directed lesson in front of the class.

The most important point about this process is that you spend some time anticipating what could possibly go wrong once you set your pupils a task or activity. Once you have done this, you will be able to announce your expectations to counteract potential pupil indiscipline. It is fair to say that the best teachers regularly use this **'anticipatory'** style of behaviour management. They spend a considerable amount of time thinking about how their lessons could be 'ambushed' and then plan accordingly.

The best teachers use 'anticipatory' behaviour management strategies.

Personally, I think Little Bighorn Birthday Bash is a crap name for a surprise catering company and Mr Custer, our very first client, will hate it.

Although I have included examples of some of my classroom routines for you to consider it is important to remember that simply taking someone else's routines and trying to make them work for you isn't always successful. You need to personalize your behaviour management approach. Take a look at the templates (see overleaf) (also available on the companion website (http://education.dixie.continuumbooks.com) and you will notice that I have accompanied each specific rule with its associated rationale. One way to fully involve the pupils in the process is to copy each rule on to a card, cut out the text describing the rationale and then ask them to match these up appropriately. Doing this will provide pupils with ownership of the process and will make it more likely that they will take your expectations 'on board'.

Rules for Group Work

You should plan and complete your assignment <u>together</u>.	Remember, a chain is only as strong as its weakest link! Unless you do your bit, the learning of the whole group will be affected
You need to appoint a coordinator. This is someone who is well organised, good with people and someone who can motivate you all to get the work done properly and on time.	It is important not to choose your friends for this role unless you know that they have the qualities required to do the job.
You need to tell the coordinator where you will be working.	Doing this will mean that the coordinator will be able to locate you immediately thus reducing the amount of learning time lost.
The coordinator needs to check that work is being done. One of the coordinator's jobs is to let the teacher know how well you are all working	Having appointed the coordinator, you need to be positive in allowing them to check your progress. After all they have a job to do. In short, you need to trust them.
Try to avoid taking work home.	If you are absent from school your peers will not be able to access your work.
Work to your strengths	We all learn in different ways. To get the job done efficiently choose something you know you can do well.
Get telephone numbers and/or e mail addresses.	It may be necessary to contact your peers outside of school hours in order to ensure that the task is completed.
Meet every now and then in order to review progress	Meeting your peers on a regular basis will help you to meet your deadlines and ascertain exactly what needs doing.

This template is also available on the companion website

Rules for working in the Computer Room

When you walk down to the computer room you must make sure that you always stay behind me.	If you rush on ahead you will disturb the learning of other pupils.
Although I am allowing you to talk, you must do so in 'whisper' rather than 'playground' voices.	If you make too much noise you will disturb the learning of other pupils.
Enter the room sensibly and sit yourself down at a computer station. Log on to the system immediately.	Getting on to a school IT system takes a considerable amount of time. Logging on immediately reduces the amount of learning time lost.
Having 'logged on', you must switch your monitors off and then turn your chairs to face the front of the classroom.	Logging on to inappropriate sites takes time and eats into the time allocated to the lesson.
At the end of the lesson make sure that you log out of the system properly and that you leave the room in an orderly state.	Research has shown that a clean, tidy and well-organised classroom can have a positive effect upon learning.

This template is also available on the companion website

Rules for working on posters

Plan out the layout of your poster really carefully. Use a ruler to underline and create borders.	You will lose marks if you have not created neat borders and if you have left big wide spaces on your poster. Make sure that your poster looks professional.
When completing your poster use different font styles and text density.	You can use different styles of fonts and texts in order to emphasise certain aspects of your work effectively. E.g. Using bold text for titles is always effective. You could use italics for quotations.
Use 'colour blocking' where appropriate.	Mounting text on coloured paper can be a very effective way of drawing the reader's attention to specific parts of your poster. It will provide your poster with impact.

Rules for working on posters *(continued)*

Include illustrations and cuttings which have been cut out neatly and stuck in with glue and not sticky tape.	Again you will lose marks if the poster doesn't look as though it has been put together with care and precision. 'Loose edges' encourage other pupils to tear these sections off the posters.
Make sure that you produce your posters in such a way that they meet the needs of your target audience. Think about who is going to read your poster, what information you expect them to be able to gain from doing so and what impression you want them to get from your work.	You need to make sure that your vocabulary and visual material meets the needs and interests of your target audience. E.g. If you are producing posters for a younger age group then you need to make your messages simple and accessible and to accompany these with relevant pictures.

This template is also available on the companion website

Don't forget that many of your pupils are visual learners. Post visual reminders of your expectations and rules on your classroom walls.

Whenever I talk to colleagues about their use of rules, routines, rewards and sanctions, most of them tell me that they do not display these expectations visually for the pupils. Bearing in mind all the work carried out in teacher-training establishments and schools on the importance of catering for pupils' differing learning styles, I am very surprised at this. It is important not to forget that many pupils are visual rather than auditory learners. To this end, it is important that you provide your pupils with visual/textual prompts if you are to stand any chance of them meeting your behavioural expectations. You could also discuss these routines with the class, ask your pupils to design illustrated flow diagrams/posters for these, and display them in your classroom. This will give the pupils a sense of ownership of the process, which is vital if your strategies are to succeed.

9 Introducing pace and purpose into lessons without leaving students behind

Introducing appropriate pace into lessons

Any driving instructor 'worth his or her salt' will stress the need for drivers to maintain speeds that are appropriate to the road conditions prevalent at the time. Similar advice could also be offered to beginning teachers who need to introduce pace and purpose into lessons while at the same time recognizing the needs of the slower learners in the class. Adopting an appropriate pace has always been an important component of a successful lesson, particularly with groups of high-achieving pupils who are more than able to cope with at least an hour of rigorous challenge. These pupils thrive on the demands of a lesson that asks them to move quickly through exposition and review to get to new learning points and to spend time developing and extending new ideas and concepts. However, it is extremely tempting to think of a lesson with 'unrelenting pace', where pupils are constantly engaged and productive all the time, as being a successful learning experience.

I have observed numerous 'all singing, all dancing' lessons where pupils have barely had time to breathe before the next activity was presented to them. In the post-observation feedback I usually commend the teacher

> Introduce an appropriate amount of pace to your lessons. Give your pupils enough 'thinking' time but don't let the lesson drag.

for their efforts and for the quality of the activities given to the pupils but then go on to ask this salient question: What opportunities did you provide for your pupils to evaluate and reflect upon the new material presented to them? Unfortunately, many teachers, even the more experienced among us, are loathe to incorporate 'thinking time' into their lessons for fear of pupils perceiving this as being 'dead time' and exploiting the situation accordingly. They work on the notion that if pupils are simply too busy to misbehave then the lesson is likely to go more smoothly. While it is true that a lively learning pace is a critical feature of a well-disciplined classroom, and if pupils are busy there is very little time for off-task behaviour, it is equally true that pupils do need reflection time. Having observed numerous lessons where the pace of learning has been unrelenting, I really do have to question the amount of 'deep learning' that has taken place. To my mind, the most successful teachers are those who are able to engender a real sense of pace and purpose into proceedings, but who also provide pupils with thinking and reflection time. With this in mind I have provided a range of guidance that will help you to inject appropriate pace and reflection time into lessons.

The planning stage

> If you are working harder than your pupils then something is wrong.

Ask yourself who is it that you want to work harder – the pupils or you? While obviously not ignoring your own contribution to the lesson, make pupil learning the main focus for all your lesson planning. Keep your pupils busy but provide opportunities for 'focused' thinking time. To make your thinking time focused, provide them with questions, conundrums, viewpoints, etc to think about. Make it clear from the outset that you will be seeking a response from them.

Have an **'entry task'** ready for the pupils to do as and when they come into the classroom. Examples of these are anagrams, word searches, crosswords, interpreting optical illusions, working out the answers to riddles, responding to pictures, etc. If you can create entry tasks that encourage pupils to get their books and writing equipment out then so much the better. This will help you to make a crisp start to the lesson and introduce a sense of pace to the proceedings.

Plan a starter activity that doesn't need a lengthy introduction but is a quick, focused activity. Again, ensure that you make it clear that this is a task for *all* pupils to do. Introduce a degree of healthy pressure on pupils to carry out your instructions.

Write the learning objectives on the board for pupils to copy down. If you want to make an even brisker start to the lesson then word-process your learning objectives and simply ask pupils to stick these at the top of the page. By doing this you will not have to wait for the slower writers to finish.

Write any homework tasks on the board for pupils to record. Inform pupils that you will be checking that they have written down these instructions by the end of the lesson. Have a sanction ready for those who have failed to do this. This sanction could take the form of an extra task or a short detention. Doing this will induce a sense of urgency into proceedings.

The initial phases of the lessons

Make sure that you move to the door to usher pupils into your classroom, welcome them into your room and remind them to pick up the resources. Scan the classroom to check that pupils are on task and not behaving inappropriately. Make sure that you are completely ready for the lesson to start and that all appropriate lesson documentation is laid out on the desk in front of you. Check that your IT equipment is working and ready to use. Scrabbling through papers on your desk suggests you are not ready to start. The following quote obtained from some of my previous classroom research makes the point well:

> Get your lessons off to a brisk start – this conveys to the pupils that you 'mean business' and that they are there to work.

> *Teacher 'X' is never fully prepared; they make it up as they go along. It's not worth concentrating.* (Year 11 pupil)

Make it your policy not to deal with individual queries until the class is settled and on task. Don't get side-tracked by pupils' requests, off-task enquiries, or administration tasks. Many pupils are extremely skilled at asking those interesting but deliberately delaying questions. Make your policy on this absolutely transparent during the establishment phase of the year.

Although it is important to deal with latecomers, you don't have to do so immediately. Becoming embroiled in discussions and/or arguments about lateness only results in valuable learning time being eroded and will inevitably result in your having to rush the remainder of the lesson. Briefly tell latecomers that you will listen to their reasons/excuses later, rather than letting their explanations delay your start.

In an ideal world I would always advise that you lay out your resources on desks ready for the pupils to collect when they arrive. However, I am realistic enough to know that in the 'hurly-burly' of school life this is not always possible. Whenever possible lay out the resources in order of their chronological use on the desks near to the classroom door and 'socialize' your pupils into picking these up as they enter the room as a matter of routine. Doing this can save so many 'break in flow' points in your lesson.

If you haven't already done so, while pupils are working on the starter activity prepare for the next activity (by writing on the board, checking that homework has been written down, etc).

The core phase of the lesson

Give your instructions for the main activity or key learning points both verbally and visually. It is important to remember that many pupils need to hear *and* see instructions before they really take these on board. This is partially in line with the traditional Chinese proverb:

I hear and I forget, I see and I remember, I do and I understand.

Where you have a class of low-ability or challenging pupils, and where you are teaching a multi-task lesson, I would strongly advise you to produce a task checklist. Using this for even the most basic of instructions, and asking pupils to physically indicate that they have completed each task, will dramatically reduce the number of times these pupils shout out: 'What do we have to do now sir/miss?' The benefits of adopting this strategy are fourfold: first, the pupils will start to take responsibility for their own learning; second, there are far fewer interruptions to the lessons; third, the pace of the lesson increases dramatically; fourth, your stress levels will be reduced! See the exemplar task checklist in Table 9.1 (from Dixie, 2007: 55). This template is also available on the companion website: http://education.dixie.continuumbooks.com.

> Using instruction checklists can avoid confusion and introduce a real sense of pace to lessons.

Table 9.1

Exemplar Task Checklist	Completed
Write the title of the work into your book and copy down the learning objective.	✓
Using the space provided for you on your 'word search' sheet, write down as many words you can find that are to do with the topic of 'Rainfall'.	✓
When you have found as many words as you can, stick the sheet into the margin of your book.	✓
Using the 'Glossary of Terms' found on page 12 of your textbook, find out the meanings of these words. Discuss these with your partner and be ready to share your answers with the rest of the class at 9.50.	

When informing pupils of the time they have to complete an allocated task or activity, do so using 'real' time. Having a fully visible clock in your room is an absolute must! It is important to give pupils the actual time when you want to them to have completed the activity (eg, 'I need you to complete this task by 10.05'). In my experience of observing lessons, teachers are often too relaxed about the times they allocate to activities.

Use 'real' time when allocating time limits to tasks and activities.

Five minutes can often become 10 or even longer. Other teachers cut short the activity before the time limit is up. I have observed lessons where the teacher has allocated the pupils 10 minutes to complete an activity and, after four minutes have elapsed, they have called the class together to 'review learning'. If pupils feel that you don't mean what you say when allocating a time limit to their tasks, they will not work at pace, or worse still will not do the work at all. This is an excellent example of where inappropriate pace has been introduced into a lesson as it has not afforded pupils any real thinking or reflective time.

To give pupils an indication of how much time they have already used on their task, you could provide them with a verbal countdown: 'You've got four minutes, three minutes, two minutes …'. Alternatively there are numerous ICT-based timers you can use to display the time on the board. Some timers will, for example, allow you to use music to increase the sense of urgency. I have known trainee teachers to use TV's 'Countdown' music to signify the final 30 seconds allocated to a task. If this is not possible in the classroom you are teaching in, simply ask a pupil to act as a timekeeper and to keep the class appraised as to how much time they have left to complete their tasks. Whatever you do, you need to be consistent in setting tasks in the context of 'real' time.

Make your expectations and the circumstances of learning absolutely transparent to the pupils from the very start, and be consistent in enforcing these: eg, working in silence. If you have allocated pupils two minutes to discuss an issue with their partner, then two minutes it should be. If you have asked the class to work in silence on a task, then have a sanction ready in the event of this not happening.

Introducing a 'competitive' element into proceedings can inject pace into a lesson.

Introducing a competitive element to your lesson can often create a sense of pace to proceedings. Having said this, you need to be very careful that the results of the 'competition' itself do not override the learning that is taking place, and that you provide sufficient scaffolding to the less able and/or less competitive element in the class.

Using fast-paced classical and/or contemporary pop music can often introduce a sense of pace to lessons. It is interesting to note that in times of customer congestion, superstores often use fast-paced music to move shoppers through the aisles and check-outs as quickly as possible. The same process can work in lessons. Alternatively, if you want to slow down the pace of a lesson, perhaps in situations where you want pupils to reflect and evaluate, you might consider using slower-paced music.

Set tasks that rely on pupils having to share their contributions with their peers, either on a partner/group basis or with the rest of the class. If pupils think that someone else in the group is going to take responsibility for making the contribution, they will be more likely to opt out of the activity. However, if they know they have to share their personal contributions with a partner/group, or that they will have to demonstrate their newly gained knowledge to the rest of the class, they will perhaps feel a greater pressure to complete the activity.

A really good way to ensure that pupils work at pace and to the best of their ability, is to circulate the classroom, and where you find a pupil not doing this, do not say anything but simply put the current time in the margin of their page. Doing this is often enough to convey to the pupil that you will be coming back to check how much work they have done since your last visit.

If you are teaching an able group, regularly ascribe the roles of chair-person or lead-learner to pupils who will then take on the mantle of responsibility and help maintain momentum and focus during tasks.

The end phase of the lesson

Make sure that you always run a plenary session. Keep the end-of-lesson plenary short, focused and pithy. Examples are:

'You have two minutes to write down two facts you have learnt this lesson.'
'Turn to your neighbour and tell them two reasons for ….'
'What has the poem taught you about yourself?'

'How can you use the learning from this lesson to inform other subjects?'
'Draw a quick sketch that represents the learning you have done today.'

Get individuals or groups of pupils to use their findings to provide the questions for the plenary and/or to prepare a related starter for the next lesson.

> Do not let the end-of-lesson plenary session get squeezed out.

If you are receiving pupil feedback during the lesson, enlist a pupil to record ideas on the board while you lead the discussion. This will allow you to scan the class to make sure that every pupil is listening and engaged with the learning.

Have pupils clear away in plenty of time and ask them to stand quietly behind their chairs before the bell goes. You need to end the lesson promptly so that you can begin your next 'pace-driven' lesson on time!

Appropriately-paced lessons for pupils require two major elements: considered planning and the establishment of systems, rules and routines. It is vital to stress that none of the strategies proffered in this chapter are likely to work if you have not launched and reinforced your expectations in the establishment phase of the year in a robust and consistent manner. My experience as an ITT/Induction tutor informs me that introducing pace into lessons is quite daunting for many beginning teachers. However, I am confident that the strategies offered in this book along with the benefits of increased experience will mean that this skill will soon become 'second nature' to you. I am also in no doubt that success with this aspect of your teaching will have extremely positive effects on the accelerated learning of your pupils.

10 Working collaboratively with teaching assistants

It is highly likely, at some point during the early stages of your teaching career, that you will be working with a TA (teaching assistant), LSA (learning support assistant) or CTA (classroom teaching assistant). For the purposes of this book I will refer to this additional adult in the classroom as a 'teaching assistant'.

Unless ground rules and expectations are established and understood by both parties, these working relationships can often become competitive and/or uncomfortable at times. In my role of observer I have witnessed numerous occasions where the teacher and teaching assistant have used the classroom arena to score points off each other. This part of the book will offer advice about how to work collaboratively rather than competitively with teaching assistants.

> Ground rules and expectations between teacher and assistant must be established at the outset for effective collaborative working.

Although teaching assistants are in the classroom in a supporting role, it is fair to say that many of you will feel somewhat threatened by having another adult in your lesson. This anxiety is perfectly understandable for new or beginning teachers because these colleagues are likely to have a far greater knowledge of the pupils and of the workings of the school. Because anxiety levels are likely to be heightened at this stage of your career it is easy to forget that these colleagues are there to support the learning of your pupils. It is really important to adopt a professional

Adopt a
professional
approach and
remember that
TAs are not in the
classroom to
judge you.

Ascertain exactly
what type of
support the TA
will be offering in
the class.

approach and to remember that these colleagues are not in the classroom to judge you. To make the most of this working relationship and to rid this arrangement of any ambiguity, it is important for you to take control of the situation. To this end I have provided you with a range of guidance that has been designed to give you a higher degree of autonomy as to how you can make full use of teaching assistants.

First, you need to make sure that you know exactly *why* the teaching assistant is in the classroom. Is he or she there to support individuals or to provide more generalized support? Ascertain exactly *what* type of support he or she will be offering the pupil(s). The following advice (from Dixie and Bell, 2009b) could cover a range of scenarios. Depending upon their specific remit, you could use your TA in the following ways:

- ☑ ask him or her to read through the teaching resources prior to the lesson;
- ☑ scribe on the board while you are talking to the class;
- ☑ act as timer and/or point-scorer when you are running quizzes;
- ☑ check and sign homework diaries;
- ☑ use an observation checklist to monitor his or her pupils' participation;
- ☑ help pupils to use the learning resources and equipment;
- ☑ ensure that pupils fully understand instructions;
- ☑ encourage pupil participation by using the prompts and questions issued by the teacher;
- ☑ rehearse answers with pupils ready for the plenary session;
- ☑ remind pupils of set targets and help them to assess their own progress;
- ☑ work with small groups and/or individual pupils;
- ☑ extend and support the more able pupils in the class.

You probably already know how important status is in the teaching profession. By 'status' I do not necessarily mean the 'ascribed' status associated with moving up the promotion ladder but rather the 'achieved' status that is gained by earning the respect of your pupils and colleagues. The same principle applies to your TAs. If you wish to avoid potential friction in your classroom, it is imperative to raise the status of your teaching assistant by ensuring that your pupils understand that you will be working as a team. It is vital that you to show the pupils a 'united front' and that you indicate that you will not tolerate rudeness or lack of cooperation towards you or your colleague. You can raise the status of your teaching assistant by following these top tips.

Raise the status of your TA and show a united front.

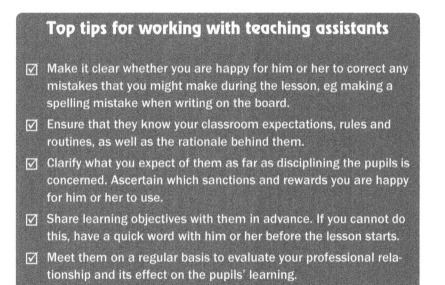

Top tips for working with teaching assistants

- ☑ Make it clear whether you are happy for him or her to correct any mistakes that you might make during the lesson, eg making a spelling mistake when writing on the board.

- ☑ Ensure that they know your classroom expectations, rules and routines, as well as the rationale behind them.

- ☑ Clarify what you expect of them as far as disciplining the pupils is concerned. Ascertain which sanctions and rewards you are happy for him or her to use.

- ☑ Share learning objectives with them in advance. If you cannot do this, have a quick word with him or her before the lesson starts.

- ☑ Meet them on a regular basis to evaluate your professional relationship and its effect on the pupils' learning.

I am certain that if you manage to do all of this, you and your teaching assistant will enjoy an extremely effective professional relationship. This is turn will have a positive effect on pupils' learning.

11 Making the school environment a positive and safe place to be

I would like to use this sign to emphasize the importance of creating a safe and secure environment for your tutor group and/or your primary school classroom. You will remember the discussion on the role of the reptilian brain presented to you in Section 1, where I stressed your need to cater for the safety and security needs of your pupils by providing a warm and stimulating classroom environment. I would like to expand on this by asking you to consider *who* you allow in to your classroom room during non-lesson time.

It is worth remembering that for some of your more fragile pupils, their form room will be their only 'safe haven' during the course of the school day. With this in mind, you might want to think about having a policy designed to restrict entry to the classroom to form/class members and selected 'others'. I would strongly advise that you afford as much ownership of the room as possible to your class members; doing so will provide them with a sense of pride and most certainly reduce the amount of vandalism and/or graffiti. Get your pupils to appoint a committee with the brief of producing an entry policy. Make sure that you outline the relevant 'issues' before eventually giving them the responsibility of coming up with this policy.

> Make sure your form room feels 'safe and secure' for your pupils.

12 Personalizing learning and multiple intelligences

The message behind this particular sign relates to your need to cater for the individual learning styles and/or intelligences of the pupils in your classes. Doing so allows pupils to realize similar learning outcomes via different routes. It is this process that embodies the principles of **personalized learning** and **differentiation.** Failing to do so can have serious ramifications on the behaviour and learning of your pupils. To cater for and challenge pupils' **dominant learning styles and intelligences,** it is necessary to have a rudimentary understanding of the functions of the brain's neo-cortex and the limbic system.

> To cater for different learning styles and abilities, it's important to understand the functions of the neo-cortex and the limbic system.

The **neo-cortex** is the newer portion of the cerebral cortex that serves as the centre of higher mental functions for humans. It contains some 100 billion cells, each with 1,000 to 10,000 synapses (connections), and has roughly 100 million metres of wiring, all packed into a structure the size and thickness of a formal dinner napkin. The cells in the neo-cortex are arranged in six layers, within which different regions permit vision, hearing, touch, sense of balance, movement, emotional responses and every other feat of cognition. In simple terms the neo-cortex can be divided into left and right hemispheres, each of which has a different function.

> The neo-cortex can be divided into left and right hemispheres.

Table 12.1 The Neo-Cortex

Characteristics	Implications for learning and teaching
This is the upper part of the brain and is thought to be associated with skills such as problem solving, language development, pattern recognition, reflective thought and creative expression. It is here that individuals create their own models and "mental maps" in order to create meaning.	Facilitate the creation of mental models by: ■ setting the work in context of previous work; ■ using novel contexts or sources of information; ■ providing input for all senses; ■ providing a variety of different activities; ■ acknowledging pupils' relatively short concentration spans.

From Gererd Dixie's lecture 'Introducing Creativity to your Teaching' 2010 delivered to Norfolk and Suffolk GTP and SNITT trainees

> The right brain is intuitive and visual – it looks at the whole picture.

> The left brain is methodical and verbal – it looks at the pieces before putting them together.

The concept of right-brain and left-brain thinking developed from the research in the late 1960s of an American psycho-biologist Roger W. Sperry. Sperry discovered that the human brain has two very different ways of thinking. He discovered that the right brain is visual and that it processes information in an intuitive and simultaneous way, looking first at the **whole picture** before exploring the details. The other (the left brain) is verbal and processes information in an analytical, structured and sequential way, looking first at the pieces then collating these to get the whole.

For some reason, our right and left hemispheres control the 'opposite' side of our bodies, so the right hemisphere controls our left side and processes what we see in our left eye, while the left hemisphere controls the right side and processes what our right eye sees. However, do not make assumptions that hand dominance determines whether you have a dominance of left or right brain as they are not directly related. And remember, just like you don't do everything with the one hand, so too your brain doesn't do everything with the one hemisphere, although there is generally a preference. The characteristics of right-brain and left-brain thinking are shown in Table 12.2.

Characteristics of left and right brain thinking.

Table 12.2

The left hemisphere	The right hemisphere
This is thought to be the analytical side of the brain. It controls the development of: ■ language; ■ logic and number concepts; ■ analysis; ■ working in a sequential approach; ■ building the whole from the parts.	This is thought to be the intuitive or non-verbal side of the brain. It controls the development of: ■ visualisation; ■ imagination; ■ rhyme and rhythm; ■ working from the whole picture to the individual parts.
Learners prefer: ■ structured tasks; ■ explicit instructions; ■ written information; ■ working in a logical and linear way.	Learners prefer: ■ open-ended tasks; ■ self-selected tasks; ■ working from intuition; ■ following hunches and guesses.

From Gererd Dixie's lecture 'Introducing Creativity to your Teaching' 2010 delivered to Norfolk and Suffolk GTP and SNITT trainees

I suspect that some of you are beginning to think about whether it is better to be right-brained or left-brained. Though right-brain or non-verbal thinking is often regarded as more 'creative', there is no right or wrong here; it's merely two different ways of thinking. One is not better than the other, just as being right-handed is not 'superior' to being left-handed. It is important to be aware that there are different ways of thinking and you need to be aware of your natural preference. Once this has been recognized, it is important to find ways to challenge yourself. The same principle should apply to your pupils.

Our current education system is dominated by left-brain thinkers and most forms of instruction and assessment are carried out using a left-brain approach, for example, written examinations and Standard Attainment Tests. As this is the case, what happens to pupils who prove to be unreceptive to traditional left-brain teaching? The answer is simple: many of them get bored, switch off and become 'marginalized'. Their failure to gain status for 'who they are' and 'what they can do' causes many of these pupils to look for recognition in less appropriate ways – ie though misbehaviour. It is not surprising that most (but certainly not all) boys are predominantly right-brain learners and it is boys rather than girls who are underachieving at every level of the examination system and who are becoming increasingly marginalized in schools.

> In order to cater for and challenge all your pupils, you must accommodate both hemispheres when planning your lessons.

If you want to engage right-brain learners while continuing to challenge those pupils for whom the left-brained approach is more accommodating, you need to address this in the lesson planning stage. One of the first things you need to do is to issue your pupils with a 'Hemisphere dominance' questionnaire to ascertain the learning preferences of your pupils. You can find numerous examples of these on the internet, such as http://www.web-us.com/brain/braindominance.htm. Having gained and recorded the results, you can then set about devising activities that will challenge and/or cater for your pupils' learning styles. This chapter contains a number of strategies that will help you to provide learning experiences for predominantly right-brain learners. Having said this, I again stress the importance of challenging the learning preferences of your pupils.

> Give your students a questionnaire to ascertain which type of learner they are, then devise activities that will cater for and/or challenge their learning styles.

Visualization, imagination, rhyme and rhythm

Imagery is a powerful force for perception and understanding. Being able to 'see' something mentally is a common metaphor for understanding it. An image may take the form of a geometrical shape, photograph, object, graph, scenario, etc. It is beyond the remit of this manual to explore the issue of visualization, imagination and rhyme and rhythm in any great detail and unrealistic to expect a bank of ideas to stimulate pupils' right brains in every subject. What I have done is to present you with some basic examples of how you could get your pupils to develop their visualization and imaginative skills, and I simply ask you to personalize these according to your subject areas. To demonstrate the power of visualization as a 'right-brain' learning tool I have provided you with some quite disparate visualization examples below.

> Visualization is a powerful right-brain learning tool.

One visualization example I would like to share with you comes from a Year 6 Maths class where the pupils were seated opposite each other and separated by a large board. Behind the board, and unseen by their partners, the pupils designed a 3D shape from a few coloured cubes and then described it. The pupils on the other side of the screen then tried to visualize this configuration before making their own version in accordance with the description offered by their partner.

This next example of visualization was observed in a geography lesson, but the strategy could be equally applied in drama, English, science, RE or PSHE. This type of visualization is called 'The Mind Movie'. Introduce the idea of 'movie shots' – close-ups and wide-angle shots. Then read an extract from a story one section at a time, asking pupils to jot down any images that they think would make good movie shots after each section. Inform the class that they will eventually have to select six of the best shots and link these to appropriate sound effects and music. Before you start reading the extract ask the pupils to stop you when they feel that this would be the place for a suitable shot. Model this process again before continuing with the story. After your general feedback/sharing of ideas, you could ask your pupils to select six prime shots to illustrate these and

> Make use of 'Mind Movies' in your lessons.

add supportive annotated text. Finally, you could get them to provide the ending to the story. Here is an example of a story that would work well:

> *Heavy soaking rain fell all through 1973. By Christmas the dams were full of life-giving water ready to be pumped to outlying farms or to the city water treatment works. The landscape looked cool, clean and green. My husband (Trevor) and I were living in two caravans at the rear of his mother's house. One caravan we had converted to a kitchen/dining room and the other served as a bedroom. We were happy there, madly squirreling our savings away to buy a home of our own. We had the deposit and were starting to look for a house. This was just as well as I was nine months pregnant and expecting any day now.*
>
> *On 24 January we turned on the news to see that Cyclone Wanda had formed off the Queensland coastline bringing with it days and days of torrential rain. Looking out of our caravan window we were able to see the rivers and creeks beginning to swell and spill over their banks. Our home was in danger of flooding and the roads were becoming inaccessible. By 26 January, aware of the fact that my baby could arrive at any time, I was packed off to stay with my brother-in-law and his wife. They lived close to the hospital. Mass evacuations were happening across the city as the water rose. Some people with foresight managed to shift their furniture and belongings. Others lost all they had except the clothes they were wearing. The flood waters continued to rise. At 2 am on 29 January my contractions started. I woke Trevor, he grabbed my overnight bag and we set out to drive through the rain to the hospital.*
>
> *What happened next …?*

Teachers of PE might be interested in using 'visualization' as a motivational tool and as a means of raising pupils' self-expectations. It is a well known fact that numerous athletes are turning to a sports psychology training technique known as visualization to sharpen their competitive edge. The technique involves mentally rehearsing for a competition, playing 'movies' of a superb past performance or the ideal performance over and over in the mind.

In today's achievement-oriented world, it's easy to dismiss the importance of imagination. My previous experience as a teacher of pupils of all ages and abilities has taught me that imagination is vital in giving your pupils the ability to deal with everyday feelings and problems. However, although opportunities for pupils to use their imaginations in primary schools are numerous, I am constantly disappointed by the lack of imaginative worked planned by teachers in secondary schools.

We process words as language in the frontal lobe of the brain. This occurs in the same way that a computer processes language. As we mature, we become increasingly able to process words in another format: as raw stimuli. This happens as we accumulate a vast store of experiences in our long-term memory. This bank of experiences could be stored in the form of images, sounds, smells and so forth and forms a kind of database that can be accessed when seeking to respond to the different stimuli presented before us.

We use our brain's 'database' to visualize. It's the 'image-ination'. It develops through use, so it doesn't fully develop until a person is in his or her mid-20s. By this time the hard-wiring of the brain is becoming more developed. Instead of merely reacting to words in a mechanistic manner, the mature adult calls upon his or her own experiences to add an emotional slant to their response. Children have imaginations too, but their imaginations haven't yet accumulated a vast store of experiences to reference and are not yet networked with words. This means that a child's imagination cannot be stimulated in the same way as that of an adult. (This is why you need to support your text with pictures wherever possible.) Experts think this is why teenagers and children show 'poor judgement'. Mature adults do not put any more effort than young people into 'thinking before acting', but they automatically imagine an act before doing it. They therefore recognize what could go wrong and receive this warning in a way that has much greater impact. If words don't stimulate the imagination, they are processed merely as 'language' in the front of the brain.

> Because the imaginations of young children and teenagers have not fully developed, they often display poor judgement when making decisions.

This information has serious implications for you as a teacher. In short, the sensory input in your lessons has got to be strong enough to evoke an 'imaginative' rather than a 'mechanistic' response from your pupils. The list of suggestions provided below only 'scratch the surface', and should you wish to explore this issue in greater depth then you need to observe a range of colleagues teaching across the curriculum and/or carry out your own research into the issue.

You could get your pupils to:

☑ sketch their feelings and/or emotions. You could ask them to support this with creative writing;

☑ draw cartoons of their feelings, thoughts or ideas or of an issue and come up with relevant captions;

☑ produce a collage to represent an idea, emotion, issue, etc;

☑ write a radio script;

☑ write imaginary letters and diaries;

☑ use random ingredients to produce an 'original' dish;

☑ produce a piece of drama and/or dance to represent a feeling, emotion, issue or story;

☑ take on the role of another person;

☑ design their ideal society;

☑ produce a recognizable object from junk material;

☑ design useful household objects;

☑ design clothes;

☑ use rhyme and rhythm to learn factual information;

☑ write the lyrics to a song about an idea, issue, emotion, feeling, etc;

☑ produce a board game designed to get younger pupils to think about particular ideas, emotions, feelings, issues, etc;

☑ respond to music extracts using a variety of media – artwork, poetry, prose, collage, drama, dance.

> Ensure that you introduce a high level of sensory input as a means of stimulating your pupils' imaginations.

Working from the whole picture to individual parts

Imagine this scenario. Having just spent a week exploring a particular topic and setting up a question/hypothesis for a coursework activity, you inform the class that you now expect them to start working independently on the task in hand. Noticing that at this point Gary has raised his hand, you signal for him to respond. 'I know the answer sir', he says enthusiastically. You ask, 'What do you mean, you know the answer?' 'I've got the answer to the question/hypothesis,' Gary states in a triumphal manner.

The point about right-brain learners such as Gary is that they are happier using their intuition and drawing conclusions from the whole picture rather than building up their learning in a sequential and logical manner. In short, Gary cannot see the point of having to tackle all the left-brain tasks required to draw conclusions about the hypothesis or question; instead he would rather provide you with a gut response to the issue laid out before him. Although there is most definitely a place for sequential, logical and methodical left-brain learning in your lessons, it is also important that you provide opportunities for right-brain learners. You can do this by presenting 'whole-picture' scenarios to stimulate intuition and subsequent discussion, before breaking down the topic into sequential, bite-size tasks that combine to form the whole. I have provided a couple of examples below. Although the number of examples provided is limited, I am certain that you will be able to apply this strategy to your own subject areas.

> Provide opportunities for 'whole-picture' intuitive learning for your right-brain learners.

My first example comes from geography and relates to the decision-making factors involved in locating a new reservoir. Instead of adopting a left-brain approach by taking each decision-making factor in turn (high rainfall, low population, easily dammed valley, impermeable rock, etc) you could use a right-brain approach by displaying a series of photographs of potential reservoir locations. At this point, ask pupils to use their intuition to stand next to the photographs that best represents the prime site for a reservoir. You could then set up a question/answer session, during which pupils have to justify their choice of location by 'making an educated guess'. As the discussion unfurls, and as new information is revealed, give permission for pupils to constantly change their minds and move to the position that best represents their current choice. By doing this, you will gradually be introducing the contributory decision-making factors in a more fluid and creative manner. Pupils will then be more prepared to take these on board at a later stage.

My second example comes from English Literature and relates to a GCSE text. Instead of starting the text at the beginning and working through each page sequentially, you could simply present the class with the final scene of the play and ask groups of pupils to produce their own 'potted' version to show how the story might lead up to this particular scene. The pupils could either read these versions out in class or use role-play to tell their story. It is important that you give full credit to pupils for using their imaginations before then positing this challenge: 'Ok, we have heard your version of the play, let's see whose version is closest to the original story.' Because you have used an engaging right-brain hook, you are more likely to have gained the initial interest of your pupils and they will be more prepared to give the play a chance.

> Ensure that your lessons have an 'emotional' input to cater for your pupils' limbic brains.

One of the best ways of catering for the neo-cortex is to provide an input for all senses. Catering for visual, auditory and kinaesthetic learners will most certainly engage right-brain thinkers and, provided the opportunities are well thought out, will also stimulate and motivate pupils with a left-brain bias. Doing this in an appropriate manner will also cater for the middle part of the brain known as the 'limbic system' (see Table 12.3). The limbic brain is the seat of our long-term memory, feelings and emotions. Research has shown that where pupils' emotional brains are engaged, learning and long-term retention is more likely to occur.

Catering for different learning styles

One of the most common and widely-used methods for categorizing learning styles is the VARK model, which identifies four types of learners:

1 visual learners;
2 auditory learners;
3 reading/writing-preference learners; and
4 kinaesthetic learners or tactile learners.

In this model visual learners have a preference for seeing (they think in pictures; visual aids such as overhead slides, diagrams, handouts, etc).

Table 12.3 Limbic System

Characteristics	Implications for learning and teaching
This part of the brain controls our emotions, beliefs and values. These stem from our identity and provide our motivation to learn. It also controls our long-term memory. This suggests that emotion is likely to be linked with memory retention. Positive emotions are thought to speed up transmission processes in the brain and so facilitate learning.	■ Raise self-esteem by: generating a "can do" culture; ■ Ensure the work has <u>relevance and where possible is linked to pupils' experiences</u>; ■ Set targets for each pupil that are challenging and yet still achievable; ■ Value all contributions; ■ Provide quick and positive feedback.

From Gererd Dixie's lecture 'Introducing Creativity to your Teaching' 2010 delivered to Norfolk and Suffolk GTP and SNITT trainees

Auditory learners learn best through listening (by attending lectures, taking part in discussions, listening to audio recordings, etc). Tactile/kinaesthetic learners prefer to learn via experience: moving, touching and doing (by actively exploring elements of the world; by carrying out science projects and experiments, etc). The model's use in pedagogy allows teachers to prepare lessons that address each of these areas. Pupils can also use it to identify their learning style and maximize their educational experience by focusing on what benefits them the most. It is really important to identify your pupils' dominant sensory learning styles by getting them to complete a learning styles questionnaire. You can easily access these by using a search engine on the internet, eg http://www.businessballs.com/vaklearningstylestest. htm. In addition to the VARK element to lessons, if you can provide an emotional slant to your teaching through these media, learning is likely to be maximized. Again it is not feasible to provide models of good practice for all subjects, so I will take you through a number of personal examples from my own practice. Study these examples, keeping in mind the possibility of using these strategies to deliver topics in your own subject areas.

Visual input

Using visual humour is one way to produce a 'feel-good' factor in the classroom and helps to gain the immediate attention of pupils. One of the ways I engage the emotional brains of pupils and produce those 'feel-good' endorphins is to present them with a visual joke, riddle or dingbat as they enter the classroom. You should be able to find appropriate jokes or riddles for your subject on the internet.

> Ensure that you provide visual, auditory and kinaesthetic stimuli in your lessons.

History – The American West
Have you heard about the 'Paper bag Kid'?

He was had up for rustling.

Geography
Why aren't there any aspirins in the rain forest?

Because the Paracetamol.

Science – Ecosystems
Why does the mushroom like going to parties?

Because he's a fungi.

Figure 12.1

Science – Ecosystems
Which herbivorous rainforest bird is respresented in the picture?

Toucan.

Figure 12.1 *continued*

Providing a visual hook in the form of a short video clip (preferably humorous) is a wonderful way to fully engage your pupils from the start of your lesson. Using a video clip to get the pupils to identify the topic for the lesson is also highly effective'. You Tube (http://www.youtube.com/) is an excellent website for video clips.

> Provide visual stimuli in the form of jokes, riddles, dingbats, pictures, photographs or video clips.

Auditory input

With the introduction of digital radio and audio-editing ICT programs, there is plenty of scope for you to make an auditory input into your lessons. Extracts from songs, radio plays, and documentaries are all excellent sources of auditory material for your pupils. One of the most successful lessons I have ever taught was based around a 30-second sound-effect clip obtained from a commercially produced CD. My task was to teach a group of unmotivated Year 10s about the characteristics and causes of anticyclones. Not exactly riveting stuff for your average 14-year-old! Rather than teach this in the traditional left-brain way, I decided to adopt a right-brain auditory approach. I asked the pupils to

> Introduce auditory stimuli in the form of radio clips, music tracks or sound-effect CDs.

put their heads on their desks, to close their eyes, and to see whether the 30-second clip evokes any personal memories. The sound-effect clip consisted of waves breaking on the shore accompanied by the laughing and shouting of children. I have presented a brief script below to show the line of questioning that took place after playing this short clip:

Me: Rachel – tell me what memories this clip brought to mind.
Rachel: On the beach with my family when I was about 10.
Me: Are they happy memories?
Rachel: Oh yes.
Me: Look up at the sky – what colour is it?
Rachel: Clear blue.
Me: Any clouds?
Rachel: A few wispy ones.
Me: Any wind?
Rachel: Slight breeze.
Me: What's the temperature like?
Rachel: Very hot.
Me: How long has it been like this?
Rachel: Four or five days.
Me: Well done Rachel, you have just described what an anticyclone looks like in summer: clear blue skies, dry light breeze, and high temperatures for a number of days. All of that is worth three marks in a Geography GCSE examination paper. What's more, all of that was learnt through your emotions!

Kinaesthetic input

Another easy way to include kinaesthetic learning is the 'Tableau' activity. Tableau in the educational sense is simply a set of frozen pictures representing a specific action in a book. Put more simply it is very much like the game of charades that requires pupils to guess the words or phrases being depicted by the actions of their peers. In terms of classroom management, this can certainly be a challenge, but provided that strict parameters and time limits are issued, the activity can be great fun and very successful. Ensure that you create a system that introduces a degree of healthy competition and rewards pupils for their efforts.

Joint approach

One of the best ways to introduce VAK to lessons is to plan learning outcomes that can be realized in a variety of ways. Allow me to share one final example from a series of geography lessons on 'Tourism in Jamaica'. The learning objective for the unit of work was for the pupils to gain an understanding of the social, environmental and economic impact of tourism on the people of Jamaica. Having viewed a couple of videos, explored the content of textbooks and relevant websites, and had a number of exploratory discussions on the issue, I put pupils into three groups (this grouping was based on the results of the VAK questionnaire distributed to pupils during the previous lesson). The brief for each group was to demonstrate the impacts of tourism on the indigenous population of Jamaica using their preferred learning style. I asked the 'auditory' group to produce and record a radio programme, the 'kinaesthetic' group to produce a role play and the 'visual' group to produce a series of impact posters. Each group had two lessons to prepare their work and needed to be ready to present this in their third lesson. After each group had presented their work in a manner sympathetic to their dominant learning style, I simply handed out the information sheets on the topic ready to be stuck into their books. My premise was that the learning had already occurred and I was simply providing the pupils with a record of this for their examinations.

> Introduce kinaesthetic stimuli in the form of tableaux, role play, mime or charades.

> Using a joint approach that involves all elements of the VAK formula is often successful.

Multiple intelligences

The theory of multiple intelligences was proposed by Howard Gardner in 1983 to more accurately define the concept of intelligence. Gardner's theory argues that intelligence, particularly as it is traditionally defined, does not sufficiently encompass the wide variety of abilities humans display. His theory purports that a child who masters multiplication easily is not necessarily more intelligent overall than a child who struggles

Plan your lessons with pupils' intelligences in mind.

to do so. The second child may be stronger in another kind of intelligence and therefore, a) may best learn the given material through a different approach, b) may excel in a field outside of mathematics, or c) may even be looking at the multiplication process at a fundamentally deeper level. This can result in a seeming slowness that hides a mathematical intelligence that is potentially higher than that of a child who easily memorizes multiplication tables. In other words, not only do pupils learn best in different ways, but they show their intelligence in different ways. Gardner's intelligences are shown in Table 12.4.

Table 12.4 Gardner's Multiple Intelligences

Intelligence	These learners might like to	Learning activities could be
Verbal Linguistic: Word Smart	Write; read; tell stories; do word puzzles; learn rhymes; memorise facts; tell jokes	Debates; role play; reading; writing speeches, lyrics for songs, prayers; word games and crosswords; use mnemonics to remember facts
Mathematical/ Logical: Logic Smart	Solve problems; do logic puzzles; work with numbers; play strategy games; experiment to test ideas; ask questions; reason things out; explore patterns	Puzzles; timelines; comparisons using Venn diagrams; debates; putting information onto a mind map; seeking patterns in information; creating outlines, storyboards
Spatial: Picture Smart	Do art and design activities; draw accurate representations; build and create models; read maps and charts; look at pictures; think in visual images; do jigsaw puzzles	Concept mapping; artwork; looking at and interrogating photographs; cartoons and storyboards; jigsaw puzzles; making charts and posters; constructing floor plans

Intelligence	These learners might like to	Learning activities could be
Bodily-Kinaesthetic: Body Smart	Move around; act things out; have hands on learning; do craft work; be tactile; dance	Role play and dance; co-operative tasks; creating clay objects; painting words, sentences; constructing floor plans; manipulating words
Musical: Music Smart	Music Smart Sing and hum; remember melodies and rhythms; listen to music; study with music playing; play instruments	Raps, jingles and rhymes; draw visual images to music; rewrite a story to a familiar tune; use music to remember facts
Interpersonal: People Smart	Be with others and socialise; lead and organise groups; resolve conflicts; empathise with others; co-operate with others;	Co-operative tasks; make group murals; group story writing; interviewing; conferences and debates; role play and dance;
Intrapersonal: Self Smart	Work alone; be independent; set personal goals; reflect and think; pursue their own in interests; be individual	Make a diary for a character; make a personal collage; listen to audio tapes; record ideas on audio tape; reflective journals; independent reading or research
Naturalist: Nature Smart	Learn about nature; identify, categorise and classify things; look after pets; know about the world and how it works; show concern for the natural environment	Outdoor investigation; naming and classifying; making collections and lists

When talking to beginning teachers about Gardner's theory, I am often minded of a young man called Clive who was in a tutor group of mine in the dim and distant past.

Clive arrived early to registration one morning, sat down, sighed and put his head on the desk. 'What's the matter, Clive?' I asked. Disconsolately Clive raised his head, looked at me and said, 'I'm thick sir, aren't I?' I paused to think before I responded, and then calmly said, 'The trouble with schools, Clive, is that they only measure and give importance to one or two types of intelligences and they usually do this through the testing and examination process. True, your brain doesn't really work like this but this doesn't mean you're not intelligent; it just means you are intelligent in a different way. I need to remind you that you are the boy who stripped my engine down last week and managed to get my car going. In doing this you showed a level of practical and logical intelligence that I simply don't have. I envy you!' It is fair to say that Clive was completely taken aback by this response but my words certainly did the trick. He is now a successful mechanic.

> Instead of asking 'Are you intelligent?' you need to ask, 'How are you intelligent?'

The implication of this story for you as a teacher is that you need to get pupils to ask themselves a different question. Instead of asking the question, 'Am I intelligent?' he or she needs to ask: 'How am I intelligent?'

To help you to use your knowledge of Gardner's intelligences, Table 12.4 provides a number of effective generic ideas you can adapt to suit the needs of your particular subject area. To make effective use of this information you need to search for multi-intelligence questionnaires on the internet and use the most appropriate version to identify the dominant intelligence type(s) of the pupils in your classes. Having done this you need to ensure that you plan your lessons with the needs of individual pupils in mind. However, please do not forget that your job as a teacher is not only to cater for pupils' intelligences, but also to provide opportunities that will challenge your pupils. So, if a pupil says something along the lines of, 'I don't like this work and I don't want to do it', then provided you have afforded him or her plenty of activities that are sympathetic to his or her learning preferences, simply offer the pupil this task as a 'challenge' to see how they fare.

There is no doubt that giving your pupils status for their intelligences and recognition for 'who they are' as people goes a long way to establishing and maintaining good working relationships with your classes. Identifying, catering for and challenging pupils' intelligence types will also have a dramatic impact on the quality of pupil behaviour in your lessons. According to Willis (1979) the anti-school culture displayed by many pupils (particularly boys) is caused by 'status-frustration'; the failure of the school to recognize and give status to these young people. Put quite simply, if you are able to praise and give credit to pupils for their 'alternative' intelligences, they will be less resentful of pupils receiving praise for the more traditional types of work carried out in school. The net result is that you will have a more harmonious and collaborative learning environment.

> It is important to 'challenge' as well as 'cater for' your pupils' intelligences.

13 Creating a broad and balanced curriculum

The failure of many drivers to heed *Highway Code* warning signs can have catastrophic consequences for their passengers, other road users and for themselves. Although the consequences of teachers failing to heed the warning signs within their profession are nowhere near so severe, there can still be serious knock-on effects on the learning and well-being of their pupils. The aims of this section are threefold: a) to explore how these command signals can be deemed relevant to your teaching, b) to provide you with advice and guidance about how to employ relevant strategies and, c) to provide you with models of good practice.

As an experienced lesson observer, I have lost count of the number of times that I have heard teachers use the following line when launching their objectives with their pupils: 'You'll need to know this, it's important for your SATs/examination.' Whilst I accept that there is a place for teachers to guide and support pupils through the testing/examination process, I am constantly dismayed by the number of missed opportunities to provide pupils with a wider and more relevant context for their learning. In the current educational climate the success of a school is measured by tallying up the pupils' examination grades, and then feeding these into a governmental set of statistics used to rank the school within the 'league tables'. In short, there is a great deal of 'teaching to the test/examination'. The net result of this functional approach towards education, is that we are in serious danger of producing pupils who can pass examinations, but who actually hold very little *deep* knowledge and

Provide a rationale for learning other than passing tests or examinations.

understanding of the subject in which they have been tested. This is particularly true in primary school at Key Stage 2 where pupils still take the Standard Attainment Tests (SATs). Primary teachers regularly inform me that they spend a considerable number of hours 'coaching pupils through the testing process'. This is also the case at GCSE level where it is constantly argued by many that a current grade 'C' is not equivalent in academic terms to the old O-level pass. Whatever your stance on this particular debate, you do need to be very careful not to make the focus of your pupils' learning too narrow. To this end, I have used the 'Road narrows' sign to highlight the dangers of 'shallow' or 'lily pad' learning – e.g. teaching to the test or an exam. In addition to the exam-based rationale for the topics under study, it is important for you to offer and explore more relevant reasons for the lesson you are about to teach.

Relate the learning to pupils' lives and experiences.

Our early exploration of the role of the limbic brain in Section 1 demonstrated that pupils learn best when teachers tap into their experiences and where they have ownership of their learning. To produce 'deep learning' scenarios it is important for you to ask the following question: How does, or how can, the learning relate to your pupils' experiences? Having asked this question, you then need to plan opportunities to do this. So for example, in the case of a mathematics lesson on 'area', you could get pupils to use DIY brochures to apply the relevant mathematical principles to cost out redesigning their bedrooms. If teaching a class about 'simple' and 'compound' interest, you could ask the pupils to research the best loans or mortgage rates on the market. Alternatively, you could use newspaper stories that describe the exploits of 'loan sharks' as a means of making a point about your pupils' need to borrow money in a responsible manner. Perhaps when teaching your pupils about the issue of 'probability', you could record a horse race and get pupils to use counters to lay bets on their favoured runner, before then running the video footage in class. This could be followed up by a discussion on the issue of 'odds and probability' along with formal exercises for pupils to complete. Perhaps when teaching a science lesson on 'electricity', you could get the pupils to find out how much it costs to re-wire a house, so that they could see how a detailed knowledge of this topic could save them money in the future. If planning a lesson on 'writing for a target audience' for an English class, you could ask pupils whether they have purchased sub-standard goods in recent weeks, and whether they would like support in writing a 'letter of complaint'.

The list of ideas is endless – all it needs is a bit of creative thinking and the will to 'think outside the box'. If you find it difficult to do this, then why not involve the pupils themselves in the process by setting *them* the challenge of researching the relevance of the topics under study. So for example, if you knew that you were going to be teaching a lesson on the 'fight-scene' in Romeo and Juliet, you could get the pupils to produce their own 'starter' activities designed to explore the relevance of this scene to contemporary life.

One of the best ways to develop pupils' deep understanding of a topic is to get them to apply their own knowledge, understanding and experiences to the work being covered. If you can make this work relevant, then this knowledge and understanding will be likely to stay with them for life and not just for the examination period.

Allow me to share one final example of a strategy I found to be successful in introducing relevance and ownership to a lesson. Although this strategy comes from my own practice as a geography teacher in a secondary school, the principles applied in this activity are fundamentally relevant and transferable to other teaching/learning phases in our school curriculum.

Before I left my post in a large secondary school to become an educational consultant, Key Stage 4 and 5 Geography courses were offered as option subjects to the pupils in my school. My research showed me that pupils chose to do the subject for a range of disparate reasons. Some pupils chose to study geography in the hope that they would be lucky enough to get one of the 'popular' teachers for their lessons; others chose the subject because it seemed like an easy option when compared to the other subjects in the option-block; and some pupils chose to take geography because they had experienced success in the subject in the lower school. It is interesting to note that very few pupils cited 'relevance to their lives' as a reason for selecting this subject in the senior school. I realized that if I was going to maintain interest amongst the

Get your pupils to come up with their own reasons for studying the subject or topic area.

pupils in my Year 10 Geography class I was going to have to provide them with a strong rationale for studying the topics covered within the course. Rather than simply 'bore these pupils to death' by delivering a monologue on the merits of taking geography, I decided to give the responsibility for doing this to the pupils.

Using the results of a **VARK** quiz, I divided the pupils up into six groups making sure that there was a range of different learning styles among them. I then delivered the following brief to the class: produce a Power-Point presentation designed to encourage current Year 9 pupils to opt for geography at Key Stage 4. The activity would be run as a competition, with their peers voting for the best two groups, before me inviting the Head of Year and Head of Department to decide on the eventual group winner. I gave the pupils six headings to use when planning their work:

1 Geography-related careers.
2 Transferable skills such as communication skills, problem solving skill, collaborative skills, etc.
3 Ecosystems and the environment.
4 Social conditions – housing, open space, amenities, etc.
5 Cross-curricular links.
6 Travel and hobbies.

Each group were given six counters which they were at liberty to use as currency to buy the support material that would help them with their presentations. This support material took on the form of website addresses, textbooks, information sheets and interviews with key staff in the school. Each group was advised to spend their tokens wisely and were told that in the event of a draw, the group that had spent the fewest counters would be acclaimed as the winning team.

I have to say that the quality of presentations made by all groups was stunning. Each team did a superb job in fully justifying why geography should be taught in schools, and why they thought Year 9 pupils should choose this subject for their options. The winning group visited the Year 9 classes to make their presentations during their option week. I went on to enjoy extremely fruitful learning relationships with the pupils in this class, and I like to think that in part at least, this was down to the fact that these pupils understood the importance and relevance of geography to their lives and to the lives of others. In my opinion, adopting a 'macro', rather than 'micro' approach towards my subject encouraged the pupils not to think about the subject entirely in an examination context.

Section 3

Travelling safely and avoiding the hazards

Using a range of warning signs as visual prompts, this section explores how these signs could be used to warn teachers of potential learning and behaviour hazards. It also provides a range of proactive strategies you can put to use in order to reduce the effects of these hazards.

Much of this book is dedicated to providing guidance on how to establish and maintain good working relationships with your pupils. It is at this point in the book that I offer substantial advice on how to use your emotional intelligence to 'repair' and 'rebuild' your relationships with your pupils.

The final part of the section explores a range of strategies designed to reduce whole-class noise levels when pupils are working on tasks and activities.

14 Integrating new pupils into the class

As a car driver, I find that one of the most hazardous situations to occur when travelling along a major road is when traffic merges from a left-hand slip-road. Although it is important to adopt a courteous approach towards others, one also has to consider the needs of those drivers already on the main carriageway. Failure to do so can result in traffic congestion and/or collisions. In effect, the whole process requires drivers to 'give and take' in what are incredibly fluid and ever-changing scenarios. Recognizing that this situation provides a good metaphor for what happens in a classroom, I have used the above sign as a way of offering beginning teachers advice about the problems that could potentially occur when new pupils move into an established subject or form class.

It is often quite difficult to induct a new pupil into your form/subject class, especially if you have worked hard to make the group a tight and cohesive social unit. I have known situations where the introduction of a new pupil has upset the equilibrium of the group and where conflict has occurred as a result of this. Allow me to share a number of strategies that I have employed during my 25 years as a form tutor. Just as you would expect drivers to display anticipatory skills when making their journeys, so too should teachers adopt this approach when working with groups of children. One of the activities I set up in my Year 7 tutor group was to get them to design an induction-package for new entrants to the class. The initial stages of this project involved pupils working together in groups to identify the sorts of things new pupils to the class and/or school would need to know about. The next stage of the process saw me changing the

> Educate your class about the importance of making new pupils feel welcome.

139

personnel of the groups and asking the pupils to identify and explore ways in which the class could make these pupils 'feel at home'. Again, the principle of affording ownership of the process led to the pupils tackling the task with rigour and enthusiasm, and I have to say no little skill. Here are some of the things the class came up with for a new entrant's initial week in school:

- A roster of pupils who were prepared to call for the new entrant and accompany him or her to school.
- A map of the school with the new entrant's classrooms highlighted.
- A daily roster of pupils who were prepared to escort the new entrant to lessons, the assembly hall and the canteen at lunchtime. They also agreed to introduce the new pupil to the subject teachers.
- A daily roster of pupils who were prepared to spend breaks and lunchtimes with the new entrant.

When inducting a new entrant into an existing group, it is always advisable to ask one of your 'emotionally intelligent' pupils to 'look after' them. It is worth noting that the emotionally intelligent pupils are not always the most academic, so doing this can afford real status and esteem to your 'helping hands' who might not ordinarily be rewarded for their contributions to school life.

It is also extremely important not to make hasty judgements about new pupils who join your classes. I remember one particular lad who joined my predominantly male Year 10 geography group towards the end of the autumn term. He was escorted to my lesson by a fellow pupil and, on his entry to the room, I saw him quickly scan the classroom and make a quick assessment of the 'lay of the land'. I welcomed him to the lesson and asked him to sit at the front of the classroom. At this point he slumped down in his chair and turned his body sideways in order to make eye contact with the boys in the row behind him. I have to admit that I found his body language rather negative and challenging. At this point I experienced something of a dilemma: although I felt I needed to challenge his behaviour, I didn't want to create a conflict scenario with this boy in his first lesson with me. I was just about to have a 'word' with him when something held me back from doing so, and I left his behaviour 'unchallenged' for the remainder of the lesson. It is interesting to note that this pupil went on to become the most gifted and motivated geographer in the group. Looking back in hindsight, I suspect that on seeing so many boys in the room, he felt the immediate need to establish himself as 'one of the lads'. Having established himself as a popular member of the class, he then settled down and went on to show what he could really do.

It is a nerve-wracking time for new pupils. Give them time to settle in.

15 Reacting to unexpected behaviour and events

I have used these two warning signs to signify your need to 'expect the unexpected' both in terms of pupil behaviour and as far as their learning is concerned. On the face of it, 'expecting the unexpected' might appear to be a contradiction in terms. However, just as a good driver will always be on the lookout for unexpected hazards – a tractor pulling out from a field, a patch of black ice, a broken-down car at the base of a 'hidden dip' – so too will a good teacher be on the lookout for 'watershed moments' in lessons. So, what exactly do I mean by 'watershed moments' and why do I attribute this term to specific key points in the planning and delivery of lessons?

In geographical terms, a watershed is the line of higher ground that divides two river basins. When the rain falls on the ridge of higher ground, the flow of water organizes itself to make its way down the slopes in runnels on either side of the raised area of land. The watershed is the point at which the flow of water divides. I very much see watershed moments as being points in lessons where a teacher's action or inaction can result in differing flows of consequences. In situations where teachers have recognized potential 'watershed moments' in their lessons, and where they have adopted proactive and positive strategies to tackle these issues, it is likely that a flow of *positive* consequences will occur. In situations where teachers fail to recognize watershed moments, or where they

> A 'watershed moment' is a point in a lesson where your action or inaction can determine a specific flow of consequences.

fail to deal constructively with the issues that arise, a *negative* set of consequences may occur.

When carrying out post-observation feedback discussions with my beginning teachers, I often ask them to identify the points in their lessons where they felt that things had started to go wrong. Invariably, most of these teachers highlight the point at which the pupils began to lose focus, or when they started to behave inappropriately. What they have failed to recognize is that there were numerous watershed moments that had occurred well before the point of conflict. Here are some possible watershed moments:

- Having low expectations of pupils *even before* the planning stage of the lesson. This will affect the work that you plan and the attitude you display towards your pupils;
- Inability or reluctance to plan a range of activities that cater for a wide spectrum of learning styles and intelligence types;
- A failure to include elements of behaviour management in your lesson plan. Where will you tell your 'challenging pupils' to go if they fail to comply with your expectations? Have you prepared work for them to do? Have you got a script ready so that you are clear about what you are going to say to them? Have you prepared a list of personalized graduated sanctions?
- Not 'meeting and greeting' pupils at the door and welcoming them into your classroom. Adopting this approach allows you to scan both the corridor and the classroom and to make sure that pupils are getting themselves prepared for the lesson. It also affords this space the status of being your 'psychological' territory;
- Unwillingness to establish your expectations, rules, routines, rewards and sanctions at the beginning of the year and/or the beginning of the lesson;
- A failure to set out your parameters *before* each activity. You need to inform pupils what it is you want them to learn, why you want them to learn this, what it is that you want them to do, why and how you want them to do this and, finally, what will happen if they do not carry out your instructions;
- Reluctance to take action at the first sign of pupil misbehaviour;

- Not supporting the school's behaviour policy with your own system of rewards and sanctions;
- A failure to gain a reputation for 'saying what you mean and meaning what you say'.

Watersheds and River Basin

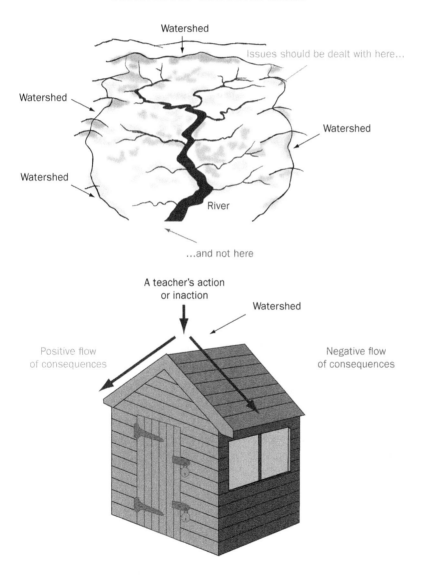

Do not look where you fell but where you slipped. (African proverb)

> One of the early 'watershed moments' in a lesson occurs on pupil entry to the classroom.

To further clarify the nature and significance of **'watershed moments'**, allow me to take one of the examples listed above and explore the scenario in more depth. When observing the lessons of even the most experienced teachers, I am often disappointed at their failure to understand the effects of the initial entry phase on learning and behaviour. Far too often I see teachers at their desks shuffling through their papers as the pupils enter the classroom. By the time the teacher is ready to start the lesson, the pupils have managed to establish the classroom space as 'their own'. In this short space of time, they have claimed the psychological advantage and the teacher now needs to do everything he or she can to wrest back that control. Although good teachers can do this relatively easily, it is fair to say that good teachers would not normally have allowed the negative consequences of this watershed moment to occur in the first place. Failure to 'meet and greet' pupils at the door is a significant and common watershed moment. Offering words of welcome, chivvying up pupils to get into the classroom, making it clear to the pupils what books and equipment they need, and instructing pupils to get on with the 'entry task' all go a long way to affording the teacher the psychological advantage over the class. It also prepares the class for learning.

> Get your peers to observe your lessons with the brief of identifying the watershed moments.

So, with this newly gained knowledge and understanding in mind, what can you do to improve your practice? You could carry out reciprocal observations of your colleagues, making the 'identification and exploration of watershed moments' the focus of your observations. Provided the post-observation discussion is carried out in a reflective and mutually supportive manner, I am confident that you will learn a great deal about how to improve your practice. Alternatively, you could use this focus to set your own targets within the 'Performance management' process. Whether this work is carried out on a formal or informal basis, I am convinced that having an understanding of the significance of the 'watershed moment' can help you to make dramatic improvements to your teaching.

16 The challenging class

No matter how conscientious you are in listening to, and acting upon, the advice and guidance proffered to you by your colleagues, and no matter how hard you work at perfecting your behaviour management techniques, you can expect to encounter **'the really challenging-class'** at some point in your career. What do I mean by the 'challenging class'? This is a group of pupils for whom your whole-class and everyday individual behaviour management strategies simply do not work. The sheer numbers of challenging pupils in the class, along with the potentially explosive combination of personality traits, make it extremely difficult to create a positive learning environment. You might recognize the following scenario:

> *It's like one thing after another; one 'brushfire' starts here, another over there! Three boys are loudly talking off-task, a couple of girls are into long-term time-wasting; a few others are walking around the room … and during the instructional phase it seems like ages before I can get them settled. Even then the students will talk to each other while I'm talking.* (Source unknown)

My main message to you is that *there is no single remedy for addressing the 'challenging class'.* Although I am satisfied that the guidance offered below will go some way to improving the behaviour and work ethic of a particular challenging group of pupils, it is important to note that in extreme circumstances the improvements may only be marginal. What is required in addition to the technical and personal strategies proffered is plenty of energy, sheer determination, a positive attitude and a clear idea of what your expectations are.

Challenging classes are those for whom the everyday whole-class strategies do not work.

There is no single remedy for the challenging class.

147

In addition to holding high expectations of your pupils in terms of their learning and behaviour, you need to be patient with yourself. It is important to recognize that sometimes there is no immediate solution to the problem and that, on occasions, you might simply have to 'ride out the storm' until such a point in your teaching career when your reputation and/or level of experience will allow you to deal with such scenarios in a more confident manner. Having said this, there are still things you can do to 'stem the tide' of disruptive behaviour and I have listed some of these below.

On a whole-class level

- Outline your expectations, rules, routines, rewards and sanctions to your pupils – make sure these are explained verbally, displayed on the classroom wall, and that your pupils have copies of them to stick in their books or folders. Make sure that you reinforce them on a regular basis.
- Ensure that you have a list of personalized graduated sanctions to support the school's behaviour management policy – be absolutely consistent in applying these. *Do not* rely entirely on the school to carry out your discipline for you.
- Make sure the pupils know that you 'say what you mean and that you mean what you say'.
- Do not adopt a reactive approach to discipline; ensure that you include your behaviour management strategies in your lesson plans.
- Ensure that you have a seating plan for the class – be prepared to change it if it doesn't work straight away. Empower yourself by telling the class that *you* are the teacher and that it is *you* who decides where pupils sit.
- Don't be too proud to seek support when you need it, but do so in such a way as to empower yourself. Arrange for a senior member of staff to come along to the lesson to support your efforts to re-establish and maintain discipline with this class. Make it clear to this member of staff that *you* would like to be seen as the one responsible for maintaining control over the class, but that you would like him or her to

witness what you are going to say to the pupils. Explain that, having delivered your message to the pupils, *you* will be inviting him or her to make comments of support. By doing this, you will maintain your integrity and control over the situation while still having the kudos of having a senior member of staff in the room to support you. Ask him or her to back you up with the imposition of your sanctions.

- Make sure the content of the lesson is relevant and interesting, with a *reasonable* level of active learning, but be careful not to provide opportunities for pupils to 'stray off task' and to start behaving inappropriately. In other words, set realistic tasks and activities. Make sure that you have more formal tasks 'up your sleeve' in case of emergencies.

> There is nothing wrong with seeking help so long as you do everything you can to empower yourself when doing so.

On an individual level

- Identify the 'key players' in the classroom. Carry out some research into their academic and social backgrounds. You can do this by talking to the Heads of Year, Heads of Department and Special Needs Coordinator if you are in secondary schools, or phase-leaders and/or senior staff in primary schools. Ask to see these pupils on your own 'home territory' during registration, break, etc – call them to an office or classroom where *you* are likely to feel more comfortable than them. Talk with these pupils and gain their perspectives on the issues. Using non-aggressive verbal and body language, outline the consequences of their continuing to behave in this manner.

> Identify 'key players' and deal with these pupils first.

- If you have to remove a few pupils from the class, do so. This is not a sign of weakness as long as it can be seen that it is *you* who is the one pulling the strings, ie: 'You can only return to the classroom once you have met with me and a senior member of staff, and when you have signed a behaviour contract.' Make sure that parents are contacted and informed of the situation. If you don't feel able to do this personally, then be in the room when the senior member of staff makes the phone call.

17 Establishing and retaining good pupil–teacher relations and moral development of pupils

I have used this sign to represent the difficult nature of the relationships experienced by some teachers with their pupils. There is no doubt that with some classes, and at some points during the academic year, you will feel that you are travelling up an incredibly steep incline. I am both hopeful and confident that the advice and guidance proffered to you in this part of the book will highlight your need to establish and maintain good working relationships with your pupils. I am also optimistic that I will be able to suggest strategies that will allow you to develop this aspect of your teaching, and on the occasions when things may go somewhat awry, will help you to find ways to 'repair' and rebuild these relationships. In offering this advice I am making three fundamental assumptions:

1 The teacher is the adult and that the pupil is not a mini-adult.
2 'Every child' does in fact, matter and that inclusion should be at the heart of our practice.
3 Our role as teachers is to teach pupils skills and strategies that will help them to behave in ways that increase their chances of being able to remain included in mainstream education.

> Remember that as adults we should take the responsibility for establishing and maintaining a climate of 'repair and rebuild'.

Whenever I deliver professional development sessions, I try to make these assumptions absolutely crystal clear to my audience. It is amazing how defensive and 'churlish' some teachers can get when they feel threatened by pupils' inappropriate behaviour. Put quite simply, we all need reminding about our professional duties from time to time. Despite the dated nature of the following quote we can learn a lot from the conclusions of the Elton Report (1989), which describes the characteristics of teachers who achieve good working relationships with their pupils:

> *(They) create a classroom climate in which pupils lose rather than gain popularity with their classmates by causing trouble. They can also spot a disruptive incident in the making, choose an appropriate tactic to deal with it and nip it in the bud. In their relationships with their pupils they always seem to know what is going on behind their backs. Good group managers understand how groups of young people react to each other and to teachers. They also understand and are in full control of their own behaviour. They model the good behaviour they expect from pupils.*

More than 20 years have passed since this report was first published, and to my mind nothing has really changed: good teachers still display these positive characteristics. Unfortunately, there are still a substantial number of teachers who have simply failed to 'move with the times'. These teachers still see the need to forge and maintain good working relationships in the classroom as 'pandering' to the whims of pupils, and regard this teaching behaviour as a weakness to be avoided at 'all costs'. What these teachers have failed to recognize is that there is a strong correlation between their teaching behaviours and attitudes, and the constant misbehaviour that occurs in their lessons.

During my time as a professional tutor, I was allocated an office adjacent to a block of classrooms in which were based a number of teachers of this type. While working in my office, I was a regular witness to the cyclical pattern of disruptive pupil behaviour that occurred in these teachers' lessons. I would initially hear a teacher 'blow his or her top' before evicting the pupil from the classroom. The teacher would then come out into the corridor to 'have a serious word' with the youngster, before issuing him or her with a formal warning and/or a detention. At this point, the teacher would re-enter the classroom leaving the pupil out in the corridor to 'stew'. A week later, and in the same lesson, the same scenario occurred with the pupil being left out in the corridor absolutely 'seething' about the lack of respect displayed to him or her. I am not naïve enough to think that these pupils played no part in these conflict scenarios, but I again remind you of my initial assumption; that the teacher is the adult and that it is his or her responsibility to deal with these issues in a professional manner. At no time did I hear any attempt by these teachers to 'repair and rebuild' their relationships with pupils. It is also interesting to note that in professional development sessions and staff meetings, this group of teachers were always the first to complain about pupil misbehaviour and 'lack of respect'. Their lack of professional and personal reflectivity, meant that they failed to identify the link between their own teaching behaviours and the conflict that occurred in their lessons.

> Adopt a reflective approach when dealing with challenging pupils.

In short, my message to you is simple: if the strategies you regularly employ fail to work, then it is worth approaching the problem from a different angle. My advice to you is always attempt to repair and rebuild relationships with your pupils by seeking their perspectives on the issue before making any decision as to the action you intend to take.

Modelling emotional intelligence

The teachers described above have all failed to demonstrate an essential ingredient of good teaching – 'emotional intelligence'. **Emotional intelligence** (EI) describes the ability, capacity and skill to identify, assess and manage the emotions of one's self, of others and of groups. In failing to recognize and address the esteem levels of the pupils in their classes, and in failing to understand what really makes 'young people tick', they have failed to demonstrate emotional intelligence. As a consequence, these teachers experience behavioural and learning issues in the classroom. Table 17.1 shows that many behaviour and learning problems arise because of low pupil self-esteem. The way to tackle this issue is by using your emotional intelligence to raise the esteem levels of your pupils.

> Use your emotional intelligence to help you to understand the esteem levels of your pupils.

Table 17.1 Understanding the esteem levels of your pupils

Pupils with high self-esteem:	Pupils with low self-esteem:
Are generally confident in new situations. They see learning as a challenge.	Are hesitant in taking on new learning tasks as they tend to fear failure.
Are able to recognise their strengths and limitations.	Need reassurance. Many of these pupils need to be the centre of attention. This often leads to disruptive behaviour in lessons. Some pupils with low self-esteem attempt to become as anonymous as possible and marginalise themselves from the learning process.
Do not give up when they make a mistake or when they find learning difficult.	Tend to blame other people and outside factors when things go wrong. It is never their fault.
Generally like themselves.	Are uncomfortable with praise. Are very quick to 'put others down' as putting others down makes them feel better. They often boast and show off. Again, this makes them feel better.
Are more comfortable with adults.	Feel frustrated that they have not been given the opportunity to 'show what they can do'.

From Gererd Dixie's lecture 'Understanding and supporting challenging pupils' 2010 delivered to Norfolk and Suffolk GTP and SNITT trainees

In addition to understanding and addressing the esteem levels of your pupils, you need to think about how your own levels of self-esteem can impact upon your relationships with your pupils. To explore this issue, you may like to consider where you stand in relation to this list of characteristics. An emotionally intelligent person:

- knows and is able to manage his or her own feelings well;
- is able to read and deal effectively and tactfully with other people's feelings;
- is able to motivate him or herself and persist despite facing obstacles;
- is able to control natural impulses and delay gratification;
- is able maintain control over his or her moods and keep calm enough to think through things in a non-emotive manner;
- is able to empathize.

Had the 'non-reflective' teachers displayed some or all of the above characteristics, it is highly probable that the pattern of pupil misbehaviour and subsequent teacher sanctions would not have occurred.

> Use your emotional intelligence to find out why certain pupils constantly misbehave.

In asking you to use your emotional intelligence, I am urging you to ask yourself some questions about your professional practice:

- Have I found out about the backgrounds of the pupils in my classes?
- Have I catered for their learning styles?
- Have I provided my pupils with a range of activities?
- Have I tried to make the learning fun?
- Have I given my pupils every opportunity to succeed?
- Have I made the learning environment safe and secure?
- Have I supported those pupils who find the work difficult?
- Have I involved every pupil in the learning process?
- Have I overtly recognized my pupils' qualities and strengths?
- Have I considered the feelings of the pupils in my classes?
- Have I been objective about the behaviour of these pupils?

If you manage to respond to all or most of these questions in a positive manner, it is highly unlikely that you will experience learning and behaviour issues with the pupils in your classes.

Give pupils a
dignified way out
of a conflict. They
will respect you
for it.

To further demonstrate what emotional intelligence looks like in practice, I have produced Table 17.2, which provides alternative responses to a specific scenario. You will note that the first response results in the pupil feeling worthless, getting angry and lashing out, while the second response demonstrates respect for the individual and gives the pupil a 'dignified' way out of the situation.

Table 17.2 Encouraging self-worth

Situation	Response: Put down	Framed positively
Everyone else in the group has finished their work except Sam who has worked as hard as he is able. It is now break-time.	Teacher says, 'What do you mean, you haven't finished your work? You've been working on this for ages! How much more time do you need!'	Teacher says, 'You have obviously worked very hard on this worksheet. You still need to complete the next three questions (stating a fact). It would be a real pity to let this go unfinished. When do you think we could do this?'

By praising Sam for his efforts, the teacher is helping to boost his self-esteem. By telling Sam that it would be a 'real pity' not to finish the work, the teacher is affording status to the work he has done. Finally, by asking him when *we* could get this work done, the teacher is affording joint responsibility for the task in hand, and is making it more likely that the work will be finished.

Another way for you to show your emotional intelligence is to make it clear to pupils that you understand the reasons behind their inappropriate behaviour. The following conversation demonstrates how you could do this:

Sally: I'm rubbish at equations!

Teacher: Equations can be tricky.

Sally: There's part of me that wants to give up if I can't do something

Teacher: That's understandable. However, it's important to keep trying. I remember when I was learning to drive and I felt really stupid because I couldn't manage to do a three-point turn. The harder I tried the more I panicked. Although I really wanted to give up I kept at it and eventually passed. Now I'm really glad that I didn't give up. Sal, I need to talk to you about the fact that you were quite rude to me during last lesson.

Sally: I'm sorry sir I didn't mean to be rude.

Teacher: Alright Sally, I suspect that you probably swore at me because you were finding the work difficult – a bit like my three-point turn I suppose. I can understand that – we all get worked up sometimes. However, I am sure you will agree that however you were feeling your behaviour was unacceptable. I too have feelings and I was quite upset about this. Do you understand where I am coming from?

Sally: Yes I do, sorry sir.

You will note that one of the characteristics of an emotionally intelligent person is the ability to remain objective and not to personalize issues with pupils. Although there are obviously going to be times when you have to admonish pupils for their misdemeanours, it is absolutely vital that you make a distinction between the pupil's behaviour and the pupil. If a pupil feels that you are attacking him or her personally, this will minimize your opportunities to 'repair and rebuild' your relationships with this pupil. I have provided alternative responses for the scenario presented to you below. Which scenario do you think 'opens the door' for future reconciliation?

> When dealing with inappropriate behaviour make a distinction between the behaviour and the pupil.

Gary is a Year 5 pupil who is constantly getting out of his seat, wandering around the classroom and disturbing other pupils and disrupting their efforts to get on with their work:

Gary, you are an absolute pain. I just don't know what I am going to do with you!

Gary, you know this isn't personal. You know that we have a rule in this classroom about not getting out of your seat without permission from your teacher. Moving around the classroom disrupts the learning of others.

> Go out of your way to recognize pupils for who they are and make them feel special.

If you think back to your own school days to the teachers who motivated and inspired you, it is highly likely that in addition to their well-developed technical teaching skills, they also displayed high levels of emotional intelligence. These would have been the teachers who made your lessons fun, who shared your joy when you were successful and who showed understanding and empathy when you found things difficult. In short, these would have been the teachers who understood and respected you and, above all, who made you feel special. Don't ever underestimate the power of emotional intelligence in the teaching and learning equation.

Understanding pupils' thinking processes

> If we want to establish and maintain good working relationships with our pupils we need to know how they think.

In addition to understanding how pupils *feel*, it is important for teachers to understand how pupils *think*. Understanding how pupils think helps us decide upon the ways in which to present information in lessons. It also helps to inform us about the way we need to react to pupils when they misbehave in class. Having knowledge of the 'social constructions' of our pupils is vital if we are to build and maintain good working relationships with them.

Although it is beyond the remit of this publication to explore the psychological theories of child development in any great detail, I feel it necessary to offer a brief summary of some of the psychological perspectives I have used in my career as a teacher of both infants and secondary school children. To do this, I would like to refer briefly to the work of Jean Piaget, a Swiss psychologist and philosopher, well known for his studies in child development, whose theory of constructivism has informed and supported the work of teachers for decades. He argues that humans generate knowledge and meaning from their experiences. He suggested that through processes of **accommodation and assimilation**, individuals construct new knowledge from their experiences.

When individuals *assimilate,* they incorporate the new experience into an already existing framework without changing that framework. This may occur when individuals' experiences are aligned with their internal representations of the world, but may also occur as a failure to change a misunderstanding; for example, they may not notice events, may misunderstand input from others, or may decide that an event is a one-off and is therefore an unimportant piece of information about the world.

> Individuals *assimilate* when they incorporate the new experience into an already existing framework without changing that framework.

However, when individuals' experiences contradict their internal representations, they may change their perceptions of the experiences to fit their internal representations. Piaget called this process *accommodation* and describes it as the process of reframing one's mental representation of the external world to fit new experiences. In short, accommodation occurs when we 'learn from our mistakes' as well as from the mistakes of others, and where, because of this new information, we reframe our view of the world.

> Individuals *accommodate* when they reframe their mental representation of the external world to fit new experiences.

The implications of this theory for you as teachers are numerous. It is vital when you plan to introduce new knowledge and concepts to your teaching groups that you identify the prior learning levels of all the pupils in your class. It is also important for you to explore and utilize the experiences of your pupils to inform your learning scenarios. You may like to do this by challenging the pre-existing viewpoints and constructions of your pupils, thus introducing the process of *accommodation* into the learning equation. Alternatively, you may prefer to build upon pupils' existing knowledge and experiences as a way of introducing new learning, in which case you will be drawing upon pupils' ability to *assimilate* new knowledge and understanding.

> Identify pupils' prior learning before you start planning your lessons.

So what are the practical implications of this theory for your teaching? I have listed a number of potential strategies:

- You could present your pupils with a series of popular misconceptions and ask them to carry out research into them before presenting the true facts about the topic to the class. Some trivial examples are: ostriches bury their heads in the sand; the term 'sushi' means raw fish in Japanese; and the memory of a goldfish lasts for only three seconds.

You will be able to identify more meaningful examples from your fund of knowledge about a specific subject. *(Accommodation)*

- You could present a series of statements in a 'True/False' activity sheet and ask the pupils to complete this activity according to their current knowledge and/or perceptions of an issue. Having done this, you could hold a discussion and/or question/answer session to clarify the true facts of the case. *(Accommodation/assimilation)*
- You could use a 'value continuum' (see page 60) and ask pupils to position themselves according to their knowledge or views on an issue. Having done this, you could launch a class discussion and emphasize the fact that you would like your pupils to change positions as soon as they hear any information or viewpoints that challenge their initial assumptions. *(Accommodation)*
- You could ask pupils to discuss a topic in pairs or groups, and to write down everything they already know about the topic about to be covered. You can then use this material to reinforce or challenge the content and concepts to be covered within the lesson. *(Assimilation and accommodation)*

> You need to become aware of Piaget's moral stages of child development.

Piaget's studies into the field of child development also saw him identify and explore the moral development of children. In his theory of moral development, Piaget put forward the notion that a child goes through three 'moral stages' on the way to adulthood.

He called the initial stage between birth and the age of 5 the 'pre-moral stage'. He put forward the view that children have very little understanding of rules or other aspects of moral development, although they begin to develop this as they near the age of 5. If you are a teacher of pupils in Early Years or Reception classes in the National Curriculum Foundation stage, you should be aware of your need to start introducing moral issues to your pupils when they reach the age of 4 plus.

Piaget called the stage between the age of 5 and 10, 'moral realism'. He maintained that within this particular stage, children are fairly rigid in their thinking. They feel that rules are important and that they must always be obeyed, eg it is always important to tell the truth ('you smell!') even if it hurts someone's feelings. Consequences are more important than intentions; eg even accidental/unintentional damage should still be punished. Naughty behaviour should always be punished. There is no concept as yet of making amends. For those of you teaching pupils in Key Stages 1 and 2, it is important for you to be aware of these tendencies when umpiring the many squabbles that occur in the primary school classroom.

Finally, Piaget identified the stage he called 'moral relativism', which generally occurs in children over the age of 10. Having reached this age, children are generally more flexible in their moral thinking. They are beginning to understand different perspectives on right and wrong. They understand the idea of a 'white lie'. They also understand the need to consider intentions as well as actions. At this age children generally feel that the 'punishment should fit the crime' and that the offender should be required to make amends. However, they do also understand that some people get away with things. For teachers of pupils in Key Stage 2 the implications of this theory are enormous. In your quest to create an ever-positive climate for learning, it is vital that you start to introduce a moral dimension to your interactions with pupils and into your behaviour management strategies.

My experience as a teacher, professional observer and mentor leads me to support the views of Hoffman (1982) cited in Bentham (2005), who purports that 'moral induction' of pupils is the best way to create a positive learning environment in lessons. He maintains that 'power-assertion' in the form of physical punishment, use of harsh words and removal of privileges has very little effect on the behaviour of pupils. He goes on to assert that 'love withdrawal', that is the withdrawal of attention, affection and attention, also has little effect on pupil behaviour. He believes as I do that reasoning with pupils and explaining why certain actions are wrong, and stressing the effects of this behaviour on others, is the way to ultimately create a positive and supportive learning environment. Having said this, it is fair to say that the degree to which this process is successful depends very much on the age and experience of the pupils with whom the teacher is working.

> Moral induction is the most effective way to change pupils' inappropriate behaviour.

Allow me to share an example of using moral induction with one of my more challenging pupils. Let's call him Shaun. Shaun's behaviour was extremely anti-social, highly egocentric and very damaging to the social fabric and learning of the class. In an attempt to help him to control his own behaviour, I used Freud's personality model. as illustrated below.

The Id stage   The Ego stage   The Superego stage

Reproduced with permission from Dixie, 2005

I explained to Shaun that in my role as his form tutor I intended to help him move from the 'Id' stage of his personality through to the 'Superego' stage. I informed him that the 'Id' stage relates to the side of personality that has a tendency to simply 'take what it wants'. This stage is typical of most young children, but can also be seen in many older youngsters. The person at this stage of their life does not have a fully developed conscience.

I then went on to explain that the 'Ego' stage represents the part of us that motivates us to commit an immoral act if we think we are unlikely to get caught. This is the stage that many youngsters in your classes will be at even at secondary school level; ie they know the broad difference between right and wrong but, given the opportunity, they will go ahead and make questionable moral decisions.

I then outlined the ultimate goal – the realization of the 'Superego' stage where a person becomes a truly moral being with a fully developed conscience and where true altruism reigns. Having done this I went on to explain that it is not as simple as the message depicted in the cartoon illustrations indicates. I explained to Shaun that humans are complex beings, and that these developmental stages are by no means clearly defined. It was important for him to realize that even as adults, the 'Id' sometimes dominates and we start to behave selfishly in situations where we don't get our own way. I then went on to explain to him that sometimes it is the 'Ego' that tends to dominate our behaviour, and that we often do things we know to be wrong, only ceasing this behaviour when we know we are likely to get caught.

 As teachers it is important to think about this before we start to take the 'moral high ground'. For example, how many times when driving have you slowed down when you have spotted a police car or a safety camera? How many times have you taken the odd roll of sticky tape from work? How many times have you told a lie to get yourself out of a tricky situation? None of us is perfect.

Of course, the 'Superego' is demonstrable in some people's behaviour more than in others. At times, most of us are capable of carrying out altruistic acts, where the only reward gained is simply knowing that we have 'done the right thing'. Although I am no psychologist, I found that this simple model helped to communicate my message to Shaun and to other pupils on subsequent occasions. Was this strategy totally successful in turning Shaun's behaviour around completely? Absolutely not! However, he did gradually become more thoughtful and self-controlled as the year unfurled, and I am confident that this approach has helped him and many youngsters like him to understand the reasons behind their behaviour and to rectify some of their more selfish traits for the benefit of the other pupils in the class. It is certainly worth giving this a try.

There is no doubt that Shaun was an extremely challenging pupil and that this was quite an extreme example. However, you can introduce a moral element to many of your everyday interactions with pupils. As long as you don't overdo it, there are many situations that arise where you can introduce an ethical approach to your discourse. Give some consideration to the following conversation and ask yourself how much could the pupil potentially learn from the three alternative responses?

> Where possible introduce a level of moral instruction into your interactions with pupils.

Amanda, you haven't cleared away. How many times have I told you to do so?

Amanda, we have a rule in this class for clearing up equipment. Thank you.

Amanda, we have a rule in this class for clearing up equipment. Paint pots and brushes should be washed out, dried and put away. Aprons should be hung up. Doing this properly will make it easier for the next person to use the equipment. I am presuming that you wouldn't want to use a dried-up paint brush or dirty apron. Thank you.

I hope that I have left you in no doubt about the importance of establishing and maintaining good working relationships with your pupils. Hopefully, I have also stressed that keeping these relationships on an 'even keel' is an extremely difficult thing to do. Human beings are not robots and we all get things wrong from time to time. When this happens, we need to think of strategies to get our working relationships with pupils 'back on track'. In short, we need to 'rebuild' and 'repair'.

18 Repair and rebuild

Picture this scenario – you are late for an appointment, the traffic is already building up and you then spot the dreaded 'road works' sign ahead. Frustrating as this might be at the time, you are likely to understand the temporary delay involved in the road-workers returning the carriageway to a safe and appropriate condition. A similar principle can be applied when, having experienced conflict with pupils, you set about restoring your working relationships with these youngsters. Yes, it takes time and effort; yes, it is inconvenient because it deflects your attention away from your teaching, but for the benefit of the long-term learning journey, this process simply has to take place.

Of course repairing and rebuilding relies very much on somebody making the first conciliatory move. I agree with the views of Bill Rogers that this 'somebody' needs to be you:

> It is up to us as adults to do the right thing.

> *It is incumbent – professionally and morally – for the adult to initiate some repairing and rebuilding after the anger-arousing incident – even if we feel our anger to be fully justified.* Rogers (1998)

Whatever you do, do not leave conflict unresolved. Kyriacou (1986) strongly advocates not leaving things to chance, and stresses the need for teachers to be proactive in their dealings with challenging pupils. You need to 'swallow your pride' and model the type of conciliatory behaviour you would like your pupils to adopt as they move into adulthood. It is also important to adopt a realistic approach to the scenario. It is highly improbable that a pupil with whom you have just had a spat will come up to you and engage in a conversation like this:

> Do all you can to resolve conflict. Do not let bad feeling fester.

Look I'm really sorry about earlier sir. I've been mulling the incident around in my mind – you know when I lashed out and swore at you. Well I'd like to repair and rebuild my good relationship with you.

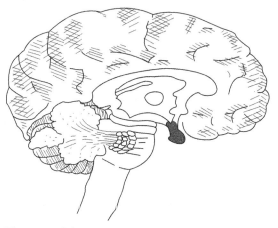

Figure 18.1 The amygdalae

When pupils feel threatened this triggers the amygdalae to produce emotional 'fight or flight' reactions.

So, why can't you expect your pupils to make the first move, especially when you deem the cause of the conflict to be their fault? You need to be aware that these pupils are not merely being difficult. The brains of most children, even those in Key Stages 3, 4 and 5, are not mature enough to do this. When stress occurs, whether it is real or imagined, the pupils' amygdalae become hypersensitive. The amygdalae are almond-shaped groups of nuclei located deep within the medial temporal lobes of the limbic brain. When pupils feel threatened, this triggers the amygdalae to produce an emotional 'fight or flight' reaction. Young children and teenagers are particularly prone to amygdalae-led behaviour. Their highly emotional responses to potentially stressful situations can get these children into big trouble at school. By our mid-20s our executive functions take over, and the power of the amygdalae diminish. We then start to respond in a more reasoned and less emotional manner.

Understanding where the challenging pupil is 'coming from' will help us to initiate and accept an apology when he or she has calmed down. You could also use this information to explain to the pupil what happens to them when they get upset, because one thing is pretty certain: most children do not understand their own emotions. Doing this will help pupils to take more responsibility for their behaviour.

How do you 'repair and rebuild'?

So, you've taken the initiative and been reflective enough to assume the responsibility for 'repairing and rebuilding' your relationships with your miscreants. How exactly should you go about this? I have laid out a number of suggestions below. Please do not feel that you have to follow them religiously; they are merely strategies that have worked for me at different times in my teaching career. Select those you feel comfortable with and which are sympathetic with your teaching personality:

> Some tried and tested strategies for repairing and rebuilding relationships with pupils.

- Allow cooling-off time – never try to solve an issue when you are angry. Remain as objective as possible and say something like, 'We are both quite wound up at the moment. Let's meet tomorrow morning when we have calmed down and when we are more likely to be able to sort this issue out'.
- Sit down with the pupil and briefly explain what it was about his or her behaviour that you found unacceptable and why. Allow time for the pupil to put his or her side of the story.
- Listen carefully to the pupil's perception of events and feelings, but always take time to refer back to the classroom rule that was broken, or a fundamental right that was ignored.
- Emphasize reconciliation. Whatever you do, do not rekindle the argument. Be prepared to go some way to understanding the pupil's anger by saying something like: 'Josh, I felt you were out of order with your behaviour, but maybe I didn't handle the situation very well yesterday.' When meeting the pupil make sure that you model the behaviours of reconciliation. Stand or sit next to him or her. Do not face him or her as this can be seen as an aggressive stance. Although

you need to make your point about the pupil's inappropriate behaviour, do so in a warm, affirming and optimistic manner. Treat the pupils with respect – you are not paid to like pupils but you are paid to respect them.

- Take one day at a time: start afresh each time you meet your pupils. It is sometimes quite sufficient to inform them that no grudges will be held, and that 'you both need to move on from here'. By using the term 'both' you are removing the total blame from the pupil and giving him or her a dignified way out of an embarrassing situation.

- Assure the pupil that despite the inappropriate nature of his or her behaviour, he or she is still accepted as a member of the class and school, but emphasize the way forward: 'You're still a member of this class Tracey, and this is what I need you to do now and in the future ...'.

- Show concern for the pupil: 'You chose to miss break yesterday because of your behaviour. I don't want you to have to miss another break in the future'.

- Discuss how 'we might handle a similar incident next time' and end the meeting on a positive note.

> Produce a behaviour plan for your challenging pupil(s).

Although I have generally found these strategies to be successful in dealing with the 'run-of the mill' conflicts that often occur in primary and secondary school classrooms, there are situations where a more considered approach is needed. Have a think about those pupils for whom your normal preventative discipline methods simply do not work. Think about how often you nag or shout at these pupils in the vain hope of getting your message across, and ask yourself whether these approaches really facilitate a change of behaviour or whether they merely serve to get pupils' backs up. Is it time for you to adopt an alternative approach to these pupils? If you feel this is the case, then you might consider producing an 'Individual behaviour plan' for specific pupils in your classes.

Individual behaviour plan

An **individual behaviour plan** consists of an agreed strategy between the teacher and the individual whose behaviour needs modifying in some way. There are different types of behaviour management plan: some are formal written documents that involve parents and other staff, while others may simply take the form of a personal verbal contract between teacher and pupil. The notion behind a behaviour management plan is that the teacher and pupil negotiate short-term and/or long-term targets for the pupil to help him or her realize these goals. It is important to remember that it is this negotiation process that is *so* vital to the success of the plan. If you have got to the point where your relationship with a specific pupil has all but broken down, you may need to bring in a third party to help you to 'broker the deal'. This could be the pupil's Head of Year or form tutor in a secondary school, or previous class teacher in a primary school. It is important to see this process as a strength rather than as a weakness!

> If the relationship between you and your challenging pupil has broken down you may have to invite a third party to act as mediator.

When creating an individual behaviour plan, it is important that you make a number of positive assumptions about the process. You must fundamentally believe that children can be helped to recognize and understand the reasons for their behaviours. You also need to believe that you have the capacity to help these pupils to improve their problem-solving skills, and that you will be able to help them to make choices about the way in which they choose to behave in the future. Finally, you need to understand your responsibility in helping these pupils explore and accept the consequences of their actions.

As you can see below, I have offered you a suggested route through an exemplar behaviour plan from its inception through to its logical conclusion. However, there are two caveats to be aware of. First, I have described the process in its absolute entirety; you may prefer to adopt a more informal approach that does not involve so many formal contributions to the process. Secondly, but perhaps most important of all, is that just because this system has worked for me it does not mean it will work for you. Read though my suggested strategies; take from them what you will, and take full ownership of any system that you find works for you.

> A behaviour plan will only work if you really want it to. It might mean you having to change your behaviour.

Stage 1: Identifying inappropriate behaviour

Identify the
behaviour you
want to change.

Having read this far into the book it should be relatively easy to identify those pupils for whom the implementation of a behaviour plan is appropriate. The types of youngsters you need to target are those for whom your whole-class management plan has not worked, and where all your attempts to strike up good working relationships have failed. I have listed the types of behaviour you might want to tackle with an individual behaviour plan:

- shouting out answers in class;
- making inappropriate comments or swearing;
- taunting or fighting with other pupils;
- constantly getting out of their seats and wandering around the classroom;
- being late for lessons and then 'making an entrance';
- talking to other pupils when you are talking.

As you are probably already well aware, these types of behaviour can have a negative effect on your relationships with the other pupils in the class, and they can ultimately erode your self-confidence and ability to teach well.

Stage 2: Setting up the process

As 'beginning' teachers, you need to be particularly careful about 'treading on other people's toes', so you must try to be sensitive to the work carried out by other members of your school team when you are preparing to put your plan into action. There are a number of people you need to consult before you set about implementing your behaviour plan. In a secondary school you need to outline and discuss your plans with your Head of Department, Head of Year and the pupil's form tutor. In primary schools you need to meet the phase leader and other senior members of staff. In both scenarios you may decide to involve parents, as they can often play a major role in helping to turn a pupil's behaviour around.

Stage 3: Meeting the pupil

It is very important that you hold a formal meeting with your challenging pupil. I have laid these out the reasons for this below.

> Arrange an appropriate time and place to meet your pupil.

Building a rapport

If your behaviour plan is going to stand any chance of working, it is vital that you use the meeting to build a rapport between you and the pupil. You will only be able to do this if he or she feels comfortable in your presence.

> Be prepared to build a rapport with the pupil.

It is important for you to find a quiet private space and to make sure that you give yourself plenty of time for the process. Try to make the youngster feel special; provide a drink (and, if you are feeling generous, a few biscuits). Make sure that your body posture is relaxed and 'open' and use a friendly and supportive tone of voice. Ensure that you outline the issues and the meeting objectives to the pupil: stress that the meeting is all about looking for a way forward and that it is not simply about you taking an opportunity to criticize his or her behaviour. Ensure that the pupil knows that you are not there to personalize the issue! Use active listening techniques so that the pupil actually *knows* that you are listening. You can do this by repeating what he or she is saying and by reframing his or her responses. You could say something like, 'If I am hearing you correctly, what you are saying is …' or, 'Let's see if I've got this right. The way you see the situation is …' or, 'It is important to know how you feel in this situation. Judging by what you are telling me, I think that you feel …'.

> Make the pupil feel valued and listened to.

Gathering information

One of the main reasons for the meeting is for you to find out exactly what is causing this pupil to behave in such an inappropriate manner. Ensure that as many of your questions are as 'open-ended' as possible; by doing so, you will afford the pupil an opportunity to explore the reasons behind his or her inappropriate behaviour. Asking closed questions will simply restrict the pupil to talking about those issues that *you* have mapped out to be the cause of his or her disruptive behaviour.

You will have gathered from what you have read so far that it is important to explore the emotions of your challenging pupil. If you are having problems with particular pupils then it could simply be because the ways in which they perceive issues are different to yours. It is very important therefore to take the time to elicit the beliefs and perceptions of the pupils. I have always tried to bring the following quote to mind when engaging in conversations with challenging pupils:

> *Atticus stood up and walked to the end of the porch. When he completed his examination of the wisteria vine he strolled back to me.*
> *'First of all,' he said, 'If you can learn a simple trick, Scout, you'll get along a lot better with all kind of folks. You never really understand a person until you consider things from their point of view.'*
> *'Sir?'*
> *'Until you climb into his skin and walk around in it.' (To Kill a Mockingbird, Harper Lee)*

So that pupils are able to modify their behaviour, they have to know exactly what it is they are doing that needs changing, why they are behaving in this manner and how things look to other people. You could use role play to demonstrate to the pupil what his or her behaviour looks like to an observer. This process is called mirroring. When using the mirroring technique, seek permission from the pupil and inject some humour into your actions. As long as you don't ridicule the pupil, doing this will lighten the mood and reduce the chances of the pupil feeling 'cornered'. As we have explored earlier in this section, your choice of language at this stage of the proceedings is vital. You will get absolutely nowhere if you simply read off a list of the pupil's faults. You need to involve him or her as much as possible in the process, and get him or her to 'explore' his or her own behaviour and the reasons behind his or her actions. As soon as you tell pupils that you *know* the reasons for their misbehaviour, you will have lost them! Ensure at this point that you 'ask' or 'suggest' but do not 'tell'. Using phrases such as:

- *To my mind, bursting into the room once the lesson has started shows that you might be seeking my attention? What do think about this? Have I got this wrong?*

Find out why the pupil is acting inappropriately.

Ask permission from the pupil to 'mirror' his or her behaviour. Do this in a gentle and light-hearted manner so as to preserve the pupil's dignity.

- *You seem to be the type of person who needs to have some control over what you do. (That is not necessarily a bad thing) Do you think that this could be one of the reasons why you don't like being told what to do?*
- *I've got a suggestion to make about why you might be getting yourself into a bit of bother – let me share this with you and you can tell me what you think.* (Dixie, 2005: 115)

Although it is extremely tempting to do so, you need to 'hold fire' on giving any advice at this stage. Explain that the process will involve the two of you working together towards an agreed set of actions that will help to alleviate some of the anti-social behaviours exhibited by this pupil. However, it is imperative that the youngster comes to his or her own conclusions about some of the possible ways forward. I have provided you with a structure for your meeting below.

> Identify the possible ways forward and agree strategies to realize them.

Setting goals and agreeing strategies

The main purpose of your dialogue with the pupil is to bring about a change in his or her behaviour. In order to do this, targets need to be set and goals need to be realized. It is very important to make these goals achievable but, if you feel that it is not going to be possible to do this all in one go, you need to break down the target into manageable, achievable and realistic sub-goals. For example, if you know that your pupil would find it difficult not to get out of his or her seat for an entire lesson, then break up the lesson into, say, 10-minute time slots and ask the pupil to keep a record of the number of complete time blocks he or she manages to control themselves. Make sure that the pupil knows that constantly getting out of his or her seat and talking to others takes away their learning opportunities.

Something that has worked for me in the past is getting pupils to use a self-regulatory proforma where, using notches on a 'five-bar gate', they indicate the number of times they have been just about to get out of their seat, but where they have thought better of it and remained in place. It is fair to say that there is a degree of risk to this system, and it does require you to trust in the individuals' wish to change their behaviour. An understandable reaction might be that they could abuse the system very easily. However, isn't this just the point of the exercise? It is important to put the onus onto the pupils as a means of getting them to think about the issue, and to take some responsibility for their own behaviour. Is this system 100 per cent successful? Again, absolutely not, but I have known it to work more often than not.

19 Regulating noise levels

I know how difficult it is to establish and maintain reasonable working noise levels in lessons, especially if you are using active learning scenarios. Having said this, it is essential that you find some way of regulating the noise levels in such a way that it conveys the message to your pupils that it is *you* who is in charge and not them! What better way to issue warnings about unacceptable noise levels than to use the traffic lights sign?

Use a semiotic approach to reduce pupil noise in lessons – make use of the traffic light system.

This is a good level of noise

Everyone is able to work well

Well done.

Keep it up!

The noise level is rising

Stop the penalties...

ACT NOW TO RETURN TO GREEN

Time will be added at the next level

The noise level is too high

It is stopping us from learning

TIME IS BEING ADDED TO THE LESSON

Act Now!

Using a short PowerPoint presentation containing traffic lights, you can get your pupils into the routine of responding appropriately to the messages displayed on each specific slide. Provided, of course, that you accompany your warnings with appropriate and graduated sanctions, the system can work very well.

Alternatively, you could do what I have seen many primary school teachers do, and that is to produce a 'noiseometer', which consists of a dial that you physically move up or down from 'Acceptable' to 'Not acceptable' according to the noise levels in your classroom. This strategy works particularly well for the visual learners in the class.

Avoid issuing rules you cannot enforce.

I am aware that dealing appropriately with pupil noise in classroom is a major area of concern for teachers of all phases. In the early stages of your career when you could still be 'finding your feet', you might be tempted to make rules that you subsequently realize you cannot impose. I have seen beginning teachers, when noise levels have reached unacceptable proportions, start to panic and issue a 'gut-reaction' instruction to pupils to 'keep quiet for the remainder of the lesson'. Be extremely cautious about insisting on long periods of silence in your lessons, as policing this can be an absolute nightmare.

We discussed the need for pupils to take responsibility for their own behaviour earlier in this section. For this to happen, you need to set up a number of opportunities for pupils to demonstrate their autonomy. Allow me to a share a strategy I have used at both primary and secondary level. On the occasions when I felt that the noise level in the class was becoming unacceptable, I would insist on 'two minutes' silence and instruct the pupils to reflect upon their behaviour during this period. If I saw anybody talking for *any reason* whatsoever during that two-minute period, I would be extremely rigorous in issuing a sanction. However, at the end of the two-minute period, I would call for the attention of the pupils, and let them know that 'we are going to have yet another try at behaving appropriately'. I would remind them about their need to use 'whisper' voices rather than 'playground' voices and warn them that if they are not able to keep the noise down to an acceptable level, the next periods of enforced silence would be five, ten and twenty minutes respectively.

The reasons why this strategy worked so well are threefold. First, it is easier to be vigilant in enforcing the 'no talking' rule for a short period of time; second, you are constantly providing opportunities for pupils to learn from their mistakes and to take ownership of their own behaviour; third, you are constantly offering a reminder of what constitutes a reasonable working noise level, and this eventually becomes embedded in the psyches of the pupils in the class.

Section 4

Direction, information and road works

The fundamental purpose of the traffic signs explored in this section is to help teachers communicate directional and/or safety information to their pupils. The more unambiguous and transparent the messages portrayed on these signs, the more likely it is that drivers will reach their destination safely and efficiently. The same principle applies to the teaching journey. The most successful teachers will 'signpost' their expectations of their pupils, and will use verbal and non-verbal cues to indicate the learning journeys ahead. Put quite simply, the best teachers are the best communicators, both on a one-to-one basis and on a whole-class level. The purpose of this section is to highlight your need to communicate information to pupils in a structured and transparent manner.

20 Making your learning journey transparent

When planning a journey it is important for you to know where you are starting from, how you intend to get to your destination and the address of the destination itself.

Continuing to use the *Highway Code* as a metaphor for specific aspects of the teaching journey, signs will be used to signify the importance of providing pupils with the 'whole picture' when launching units of work and/or individual lessons. Failure to do so can result in a lack of pupil focus and concentration and subsequent disruption in the classroom. Earlier in Section 1 we discussed the importance of ensuring continuity and progression when producing schemes of work. In this section I would like to stress your need to make this continuity and progression transparent to your pupils. In other words, you need to: tell them what they will be learning; why they will be studying particular topic areas; how they will be learning this new material; when and how they will be assessed; and what you expect the learning outcomes to be. I have provided you with a number of strategies you could use to make the learning journey transparent:

> When launching a scheme of work with your classes provide pupils with the whole picture.

- You could provide pupils with flowcharts for the unit of work being studied. These could plot out the topics, the objectives being set, the activities/tasks to be undertaken, the assessment strategies to be employed, the points at which assessment will take place and the eventual outcomes you expect to be realized. Doing this will help pupils to identify and explore the links between the subject-related elements covered within the unit of work.

- You could ask pupils to sequence a series of cards, each of which contains an element of the information plotted on the flowchart. Getting pupils to sequence these elements into chronological order will help to provide them with an understanding of the integrated nature of the learning journey, and give them ownership of the process.
- The final strategy I would like to offer relates to the discussion that took place in Section 1 on 'questioning', and which focuses on your need to get your pupils to ask questions. You could provide pupils with an outline of the topics to be studied, and then get them to come up with a list of questions they might like to ask about them. Having done this, you could use a more detailed flowchart to explain how the unit of work fits together, and how their questions will be answered.

21 Communicating the aims and objectives of the lesson and setting targets

The idea of using the 'dual carriageway' metaphor as a teaching tool first came to me on my journey along the challenging trunk road initially described in the Preface. I use the term 'challenging' because although this road has been designated as an 'A Road', the route is mainly single carriageway and is punctuated by a range of different speed restrictions. Because the area is predominantly rural in nature, a great deal of the journey is spent trying to overtake agricultural traffic. On this particular journey, I had been stuck behind a tractor for about 10 miles. I was unable to overtake it for a number of reasons: it was raining and visibility was extremely poor; the road was very narrow and winding; and the 30 mile an hour speed limit simply restricted my opportunity to do so. I had just about reached the 'end of my tether' when I observed the sign indicating that there was 'dual carriageway ahead'. Because I knew that I only had to drive for another couple of miles before being able to overtake, I became more sanguine about the challenging nature of my journey.

It was at this point that I began to think about the similarities between this journey and some of the learning journeys I had undertaken with my teaching groups. If something as simple as a 'dual carriageway' sign had been so successful in alleviating the frustration and anxiety that had built up during the journey, then perhaps I could use the same strategy to rid my pupils of some of the anxiety and frustrations they experience in lessons. In every lesson from that point onwards, I made sure that I 'sign-posted' to my pupils the various activities and tasks planned. The rationale behind this strategy is that if pupils assume that I am simply going to talk *at* them for the entire lesson it will not be long before they 'switch off'. If I use the metaphorical 'dual carriageway' sign to outline the learning journey and the range of activities planned for them, they are more likely to focus and to 'remain on task'. I have produced a fictitious script to exemplify the importance of signposting the lesson journey to pupils:

> *We have explored the learning objectives for the lesson but what I want to do now is to signpost the learning journey. In a minute I am going to launch the topic for today's lesson. Don't worry folks, I am not going to talk to you for the entire 90 minutes. This part of the lesson will only take about 10 minutes to get through but it is really important for you to give me your full attention for this brief period of time. I know that some of you find it difficult to focus for very long but you really need to take this new material 'on board' so that you are able to do the set tasks later in the lesson – so really make an effort to 'stay with me'. After 10 minutes I am going to ask you to get into pairs and get you to watch and take a few notes on a 10-minute video clip. Once you have done this, I am going to give you all a True/False quiz to do and I will award a small prize to the pupils who get all of these questions right. Following this you are going to use your creative skills along with the knowledge you have gained in this lesson to produce an impact poster for X. I will spend the final 10 minutes of the lesson checking on your understanding of the learning carried out today. Hopefully you will see that I have planned the lesson so that there is at least one activity that meets your preferred learning style.*

Share the learning journey with your pupils at the start of the lesson.

22 Teaching life skills

If you have been unfortunate enough to have approached the Gravelly Hill Interchange (otherwise known as 'Spaghetti Junction') just outside Birmingham during the rush hour, you will certainly have an understanding of what I mean by the term 'motorway stress'. The number of 'entrance' and 'exit' slipways to and from the motorway is overwhelming, and it is easy to become pressurized into making rash decisions and into making a wrong turning. In the same way, there will be times in your career when you will feel bombarded by the number of demands made upon you as a teacher, and when you will simply not know 'which way to turn'.

I have used this 'multi-junction' approach sign to demonstrate that teachers regularly have to deal with administrative demands at times when they really feel that they should be focusing on the 'nuts and bolts' of teaching (preparing lessons, marking, evaluating, etc). Having said this, there are strategies you can employ to reduce these feelings of powerlessness and impotency. I have provided you with some advice and guidance on how to cope with the stress associated with these demands, while at the same time not lowering your expectations of your pupils' work.

> There will be times when you will really feel under pressure – you are not alone.

Top tips for coping with stress

- When you start at your school in September, ensure that you use the school calendar to identify the potentially stressful points that are likely to arise during the school year. Think creatively

> Use peer-assessment to reduce your marking load at particularly stressful times of the year.

about how you can reduce your workload during these busy periods. There will be times when, for example, you know that you will have to write reports, when will you have to attend parents' consultation evenings, or when you need to mark mock examinations or SATs, so you need to do what you can to protect yourself without giving the pupils a 'raw deal'. During this period of heightened activity, you could introduce a number of peer-assessment activities into your lessons. Alternatively, you could set research-based homework tasks that require the pupils to make *verbal* feedback in lessons, rather than asking them to produce written responses. Doing this will help to reduce your marking load until such time when you feel able to revert back to setting and marking written work in the expected manner.

> Think ahead, prioritize and, if you have to, negotiate deadlines where possible.

- During times of stress and heavy workload, it is important for you to learn to prioritize. List the various tasks to be completed in order of their deadlines. Although by its definition a deadline appears to be immovable, you will find that some are indeed subject to negotiation. For example, if you have a deadline to hand your tutor group or class reports into the Head of Year, it might be worth explaining your predicament to him or her and requesting an extra couple of days to complete your part of the process. After all, the Head of Year is not going to be able to complete all the reports at once so you will not be holding things up. However, it is a professional given that you do not miss deadlines without extending the courtesy of talking through the issues with the members of staff concerned.

- Don't be afraid to ask for help every now and then. There will be times when, for personal or professional reasons, you will fall behind with your workload. Provided you have built up a degree of professional trust with your colleagues, you will find that they will be sympathetic to helping you out if you are in trouble. Even as an experienced professional tutor I have occasionally had to have a day off school to catch up with writing trainee reports while colleagues have very kindly taken my lessons. Provided that, a) you do not make a habit of it and, b) you reciprocate your colleagues' kindness from time to time, there is nothing wrong with doing this.

23 When, where and how to seek help without losing face

Let's face it – teaching is an exhausting and all-consuming profession. In order to teach creatively and effectively, teachers need to be fresh and 'at the top of their game'. There will be times when you will need to pull into a metaphorical 'pit stop' to re-fuel and to recover your enthusiasm, motivation and energy. It is therefore important for you to recognize when you get to the point where you are physically and emotionally struggling, and when you need to seek help from colleagues. This part of the book provides guidance on when, where and how to seek help from colleagues while at the same time maintaining your professional dignity and status.

> If you are really struggling, don't 'soldier on'. Seek support as early as possible.

You need to prepare yourself for periods of extreme self-doubt during your teaching career; it would be surprising if you did not occasionally question your competence in being able to do the job properly, or indeed whether you really want to teach. Rest assured that other more experienced teachers will have probably had similar self-doubts at some point during their career; this is why it is so important to talk openly to trusted colleagues about the issues that may be troubling you.

Do not 'throw a sickie' just because things get tough. Experience shows that running away from your problems will not solve anything. However, if you do feel that the pressures of meeting the many demands of the job

Don't feel that you have to use your immediate line manager for support.

are beginning to have an adverse effect on your health and on your ability to make sound judgements, you need to speak to a trusted and senior colleague about it. You will note that I have been non-specific about the rank of the senior colleague, simply because as we all know our immediate line manager may not always be the most supportive of colleagues. Having said this, I do need to stress your need to talk to someone who has sufficient status and/or influence to effect the level of supportive action that you will need in these circumstances.

It is fair to say that self-doubt may not be the only issue troubling you. You will know that stress is a common problem within the teaching profession, and it is important that you take this into consideration when planning your work/life balance. Although we all need a degree of stress to perform well, there is a limit to how much we can tolerate. You are highly likely to find yourself feeling stressed in training/teaching-based situations when you are:

- unable to meet your assignment and/or task deadlines;
- anxious about meeting the required standards of the training programme or induction year;
- worried about teaching a particularly challenging class;
- in a school that does not provide you with enough support;
- struggling to keep up with the work load.

We tend to get stressed when we feel that we do not have control over our own work load.

When asked about what causes stress, many people respond by saying that it occurs when they have been given too much work to do. However, I feel there is far more to it than this. I do not necessarily feel that stress is caused by the *amount* of work we have to do, but that it is more down to a lack of control and ownership of our work load. It is important that you make yourself fully aware of the potential signs of stress so that you can nip them early in the bud. Signs of stress include:

- frequent headaches;
- exhaustion;
- insomnia;
- a feel of powerlessness and lack of control;
- panic attacks;

- crying at inappropriate times;
- feeling inadequate and depressed.

If you do accept the premise that stress is caused by a feeling of impotence and a lack of control over your work load, then hopefully you will be receptive to the fact that there will be things you can do to improve your situation. I offer a number of suggestions below:

- Improving your personal organization is absolutely crucial. If you have an essay or an assignment to do, or reports to write, consult your calendar and give yourself plenty of time to plan and complete your tasks. In the case of assignments, it is worth aiming to get your work completed one week before the deadline, because as Murphy's Law states, 'if something can go wrong it will' and doing this will afford you a degree of leeway. Starting your assignments before everybody else will also give you a head start when it comes to finding books and journals in the library. When preparing reports, you need to build checking and amending time into your planning. I would always suggest that you give your reports to someone reliable to check; it is only reasonable that you give them at least a couple of days to do this.

> It is important to get the control back.

- Before you leave school each day make sure that you have a pretty good idea of what you will be teaching the next day.
- Plan out your week carefully. If you are a morning person, go to bed early, get a good night's sleep, get into school early and do the main bulk of your preparation and/or marking before lessons start. Conversely, if you work better at the end of the day, stay on at school and get your work done before you go home.
- Make sure that you plan some leisure-time activities into your week.
- You cannot possibly do everything perfectly. Learn to prioritize and don't get diverted by interesting but futile side issues.
- If you feel that you are suffering from stress, seek medical help and inform your school mentor and/or your external tutor/mentor/supervisor that you have done so. I can assure you that your colleagues would prefer to know that you are feeling 'under the weather' earlier rather than later. Procrastination on your part might eventually call into question your ability to finish the course.

If you are a teacher trainee be realistic about your self-expectations during your course.

- Treat the feedback you receive during your school practices and/or in your NQT year as preparation for your teaching and not merely as a means of obtaining a good teaching grade. Be prepared to experiment. If things go wrong it really doesn't really matter as, at this stage of your career, no one will be expecting you to get everything right. Trainees or NQTs who have never received an unsatisfactory grade for a lesson will have probably resorted to playing safe rather than having really challenged themselves. Even if a lesson goes completely awry, you will be able to learn something from the experience just as long as you adopt a reflective and positive approach. Adopting a more sanguine approach to making mistakes will certainly go a long way in helping to reduce your stress levels.

- Be both proactive and reflective in your training/NQT year. Your mentor will really appreciate your coming to the table with a balanced evaluation of your progress and/or lesson. By doing this you will be able to exercise some control over the feedback process.

24 Making decisions

During my time as a professional tutor I have observed numerous situations where teachers have ignored or failed to recognize 'watershed moments' in lessons and where they have made inappropriate decisions that have resulted in them being backed into a corner. I have used the 'No-through road' sign as a catalyst for exploring the decision-making process, and for providing advice to those teachers who frequently find themselves in a professional cul-de-sac.

> Learning to recognize 'watershed' moments will help reduce conflict with pupils.

Making use of the tactical pause and 'take-up time'

One of the main reasons why pupils push their teachers 'into a corner' is simply because they feel threatened. In Section 1 we discussed how the reptilian brain becomes fully activated when presented with 'fight or flight' scenarios. Finding themselves in situations of potential conflict can put your pupils into 'fight' mode.

If you want your pupils to learn how to behave and to take your expectations on board, you need to model an effective and assertive way of managing conflict. Although it is important to re-emphasize your expectations and challenge pupils when they 'overstep the mark', you need to do so in a non-threatening manner. If you stand over your pupils wagging your finger and giving them 'what for', it is highly unlikely that you will be able to 'repair and rebuild' your relationship with these youngsters.

While you need to make your point about the inappropriate nature of their behaviour, it is also important for you to provide your miscreants with a dignified exit from the situation. To this end I would fully support Rogers' (1998: 57) view that this is an appropriate time to use what he calls **'tactical pausing'** and **'take-up time'**. Using these strategies properly can help you to gain the full attention of the class when communicating important messages to your pupils.

> You need to give your pupils a dignified way out of a conflict scenario. Making use of the 'tactical pause' is a great way of doing this.

Refer to the pupil(s) by name before then making full use of the dramatic (tactical) pause. Scan the classroom, making sure that you have the full attention of the class before going on to issue your instructions. The purpose of the tactical pause is twofold: to create the optimum degree of tension required to convey to the pupils that they need to stop what they are doing; and to provide a level of status to the message being delivered.

Once you have used the tactical pause you need to support this by using 'take-up time'. Having gained eye contact with the pupils, and having issued your instructions, you need to turn away, giving them time to carry out your demands in a dignified manner. Maintaining eye contact for too long in situations such as this tends to be confrontational and often brings about unacceptable defensive secondary behaviour. It is this secondary behaviour that often leads to a 'no-win' situation for both of you. You will be amazed at how using such simple techniques can lessen your need to 'wield the big stick' to gain control over the pupils in your classes. In short, using these techniques creates an 'I win, you win' scenario.

Using the language of choice

> The most successful teachers are those who do everything they can to direct pupils to take responsibility for their own behaviour.

One of the best ways to avoid being 'pushed into a corner' by your pupils is to use the **language of choice.** The most successful teachers are those who do everything they can to direct pupils to take responsibility for their own behaviour. They manage to do this by using language that emphasizes pupils' choices rather than the teacher's threat. Allow me to share two scenarios which fully demonstrate the use of 'choice direction'. The first scenario relates to Michael, a Year 9 pupil who is reluctant to put his mobile phone away. The second scenario focuses on Lisa, a Year 5 pupil who has a tendency to get up and wander around the classroom when she should be working at her desk.

Scenario 1

Teacher: Hi Michael, I see you've got a phone there. Is it new?

Michael: Yes, I got it for Christmas.

Teacher: It's a really nice phone, Michael. Looks like it's got all the latest gadgets on it, but you know the rule about not having phones out in class. Be a good lad and put in your bag. Thank you. Or if you like, you could give it to me and collect it at the end of the day. (Said in a matter-of-fact but nevertheless expectant manner.)

Michael: No you're alright sir, I'll put it away. Michael rather reluctantly slips the phone into his bag.

Scenario 2

Teacher: Lisa, could I have a quick word with you. Thank you.

Lisa: Yes, miss.

Teacher: I've noticed that you have been out of your seat on three occasions already during the lesson. I need to remind you about the class rule about staying in your seat while you are doing this kind of work. Lisa, you have a choice – you can either go back to your place and remain seated until the end of the lesson or, if you prefer, you could move your chair up to my desk and work there. I am happy with either of these choices just as long as you get your work done. What would you prefer to do Lisa?

Lisa: I would rather work at the table with my friends, miss.

Teacher: That's fine Lisa, but I will come over to see how you are getting on. If I feel that you haven't done enough work, you and I can work on this at break time. Again, you have a choice.

Using the 'language of inevitability'

I first heard this term when I was listening to a Radio 4 documentary exploring the film scripts for the 'Good, Bad and Ugly' movie series. The presenter went to great lengths to explain how the body language, voice

When using the 'language of inevitability' a teacher conveys the expectation to his or her pupils that they will comply with his or her expectations.

tone and eye contact of the Clint Eastwood character left the viewer in no doubt as to the seriousness of his intentions. In other words, when watching the movie, the viewer gets the message that the character 'says what he means and means what he says'. The presenter called this approach 'using the language of inevitability'. I really liked the idea of linking this analogy to the teaching process and began to use the term **'language of inevitability'** in my training sessions as a way of stressing the teacher's need to convey his or her expectation to pupils in a transparent and assertive manner. To this end I provided the delegates to my 'Taking effective control' lecture in 2010 with the following definition of the 'language of inevitability' in a teaching context:

> *Teachers demonstrate the 'language of inevitability' when they use assertive language to address pupils, and when they adopt an assertive body posture and tone of voice in order to convey an expectation of their pupils to comply with their instructions.*

This definition is fully supported by the work of Kyriacou (2007: 87) who also stresses the need for teachers to adopt an assertive approach to their behaviour management. He writes:

> *Behaving as though you have status will be conveyed by your appearing relaxed, self-assured and confident, as indicated in particular by your tone of voice, posture, facial expression and use of eye contact.*

It is fair to say that using the language of inevitability is difficult enough even when your confidence levels are relatively high, so I do realize how much I am asking of you as beginning teachers. Unfortunately, there is no way around this situation. If you want to be successful in creating a positive climate for learning and avoid being sidetracked by pupils' secondary behaviour, then you need to do everything you can to demonstrate confidence in yourself as a teacher. For many of you this will simply mean faking it!

25 Parental engagement

Establishing and maintaining effective working relationships with parents and guardians is an integral part of a teacher's role. This can either be done through the medium of parents' consultation meetings, or through personal contact via a letter or telephone call home. This chapter explores the issues relating to working with parents and offers advice and guidance on how to cope with challenging situations that may arise during the course of the dialogue.

If you are a teacher trainee it is highly unlikely that you will be expected to play a dominant role in the parents' consultation process. Unless your host teacher is absent, your contribution will probably be a 'shadowing' and/or supportive role. However, experience shows me that by the time trainees reach their final practice many of them are asked to make a significant contribution to proceedings and even to lead the meetings with selected parents. Most other beginning teachers are expected to 'fly solo' when attending parents' consultation sessions.

I am fully aware that parents' consultation sessions can be a time of potential anxiety for teachers of all levels of experience. Often it is the fear of the unexpected that leads to this anxiety. With this in mind I have prepared a number of guidance points designed to empower yourself in these meetings and to help you to take more control of the agenda.

> Parents' consultation sessions can cause anxiety in some teachers. Rigorous planning and preparation can reduce this.

Preparation is everything!

- The first thing you need to do is to clarify in your own mind the exact purpose of these consultation sessions. They are not solely there for you to demonstrate your excellent interactive skills, although of course they will provide opportunities for you to do so. The purpose of consulting with parents is to nurture the home/school partnership and use these relationships ultimately to improve your pupils' learning.
- Find out exactly who is coming to see you. Bearing in mind the high rate of marriage breakdowns, it is almost inevitable that you will be meeting partners, step-parents, grandparents and other relatives.
- Find out from more experienced staff if any of the parents you are seeing can be difficult – and the best way to deal with them.
- Prepare notes on each of the children you teach and support this with their prior attainment data.
- If possible check back to the pupil's previous report – it is embarrassing if your comments are very different from what has gone before, unless you have firm evidence to support this change of stance.
- Post a list of appointment times in a visible place. If parents are aware that there are others waiting, they will be more ready to stick to the schedule. Even if parents are late, make sure you stick to the order displayed on the appointment sheet. They may have been held up in other parts of the school and their lateness is probably not their fault.
- See if you can predict the issues that might arise and prepare some answers beforehand.
- Try to look confident even if you don't feel it. Remember, most parents will be nervous too.

> Having a structure for your meetings can prevent them from overrunning.

Suggested structure

Introduction: 'Hello, you must be X's mum' or, 'You've come to talk about X' (don't use a surname unless you are sure of it, can pronounce it and know the person's title).

Headline: for example, 'X has settled in well and is making good progress.'

Strengths (social and academic): 'I'm particularly pleased with ...' (have a clear example to illustrate your point).

Areas for improvement (social and academic): 'However, X still needs to work on ...' (again, have some illustrations).

Parents' views: 'How do you feel that things are going in this subject? Do you have any worries?' (Make a note of their concerns.) If this discussion goes on for too long, say something like, 'Can I suggest that we make another appointment to discuss this? I'm afraid there are a lot of people waiting.' If you are worried about the possible nature of this further meeting, discuss your concerns with your head of department or Head of Year, who will be able to offer you advice and support.

Parental help: 'Could you make sure that X practises ...'.

Conclusion: Look at your watch, smile, stand up and offer a handshake. 'Well' thank you very much for coming, it was good to meet you.'

Helpful hints

- Remember that parents want to know that you care about their child. Put their minds at ease by saying something positive about the pupil.
- Always try to be objective. Make sure you separate the work ethic and/ or behaviour from the child's personality. Do not use an acerbic tone of voice to make a point about the pupil. You are more likely to get somewhere if you offer your criticism in a warm and affirming manner.
- Have a programme of appointments with you – this will prevent you getting confused and talking about the wrong child. (It has happened!)
- Keep a clock or watch on the table – try to be politely ruthless; a slight delay with some pupils may lead to massive backlogs.
- Have a notebook in which to record the things you said you would do. If you have promised to follow up on an issue then make sure that you do it.

> Keep the meeting positive, informative and constructive.

- Do not be afraid to ask for advice or support from colleagues during the evening if you need it.
- Celebrate your success when it's over!

Dealing with difficult parents

There is a big difference between challenging parents and difficult ones. The former may put you on the spot by asking challenging and searching questions about their children's progress, but do so in a spirit of collaboration and cooperation. Difficult parents, however, are those who usually come to the meetings 'spoiling for a fight'. In the early stages of your career, it is unwise to deal directly with these parents, so get a more senior member of staff to handle the situation. The guidance that follows has been offered as a means of informing your NQT year and beyond:

> There is a difference between difficult parents and challenging ones. They need to be dealt with in very different ways.

- Refer any complaints to your head of department or a senior member of staff and ask them to deal with the situation without you in the room.
- If you have made a mistake, admit it and then allow your head of department to sort this out for you.
- Develop your listening skills by allowing parents to have their full say. Many problems arise because of parents' frustrations that they are simply not being listened to. Do not get defensive and do not bear a grudge. You have to show them that you are better than this!
- Make sure that you are clear in your own mind about the reasons behind your actions and behaviour. This will allow you to convey your perspective to the parents.
- Stay calm and do not get drawn into arguments. Repeat your own version of events and justify this in a professional manner. Avoid confrontation wherever possible but know when it is important to repeat your position in an assertive manner. If parents become aggressive or raise their voices, make full eye contact with them and say calmly and authoritatively, 'I am not prepared to conduct this interview under these conditions. If you feel that you cannot talk to me in a civilized manner, I will have to terminate proceedings.' If they do

not calm down, stand up and open the door. If they still refuse to go, leave the room and find your head of department or mentor.

- Try to understand alternative perspectives even if you do not agree with them. There is nothing wrong in saying something like, 'I can certainly see where you are coming from, but in my professional opinion ...'.
- Be the one to rebuild bridges. This is very difficult to do, especially if we feel that parents have really got us wrong. As professional people we are often better able to reopen channels of communication after a difficulty.
- Try to end the meeting on a positive note. Make sure that the parents know that you are still interested in their child by saying something like, 'Please don't feel you have to wait for another parents' evening to discuss X's progress. Just give me a ring and you can come up to the school at any time.'
- Use your experiences in dealing with challenging parents as learning opportunities. If you feel that you did not do yourself justice in your meeting, then ask the simple question, 'What would I do differently next time? (Dixie, 2009a and b)

Informal contact with parents

Although as a beginning teacher you might be somewhat reluctant to make individual contact with parents or guardians, you need to be aware that doing so can have really positive effects on your working relationships with your pupils. If you want your contact with parents/guardians to be most meaningful I would always advise that you initially make telephone calls or write letters home about positive issues. You may feel that a pupil's behaviour has recently improved, you may want to reward him or her for making a really big effort to participate in a question/answer session, or you may want to celebrate the fact that the child has worked particularly hard at a piece of homework.

> Make as many positive referrals home as possible.

Even something as simple as sending home school 'celebration' postcards can really help to boost your pupils' self-esteem, motivation and work rate. The 'feel good' effect is even more positive if the reward system has been personalized by you. When I was teaching I would send an 'Oven glove' award postcard to the parents of those children whose work was simply 'too hot for me to handle'. Demonstrating that you are always prepared to accentuate the positive will stand you in good stead should you have to contact parents about their child's inappropriate behaviour or lack of work.

If you have to make a negative phone call to parents, make sure that you speak to a senior member of staff first, as he or she may have some 'contextual' information that you need to be aware of. It is always worth preparing a script and running this by the Head of Year or phase leader before making the call. If you don't feel particularly confident about doing this, have them in the room to support you while you make the phone call. In the same way that you would endeavour to begin a parents' consultation interview with a positive comment, make sure that you commence your telephone call in this manner. Even though they may be receiving 'bad news', most parents are very appreciative of the fact that you have taken the time and trouble to contact them during the school day. They usually welcome the opportunity to work closely with the school for the benefit of their child.

> If you have to make a negative phone call home, make sure that you get permission and support from a senior member of staff.

Conclusion

I wrote this book because of my strong interest in all issues relating to the teaching and learning journey. The very nature of the title affirms my belief that this book is of real practical value, not only to 'beginning' teachers but also to professional tutors, teacher trainers and those experienced professionals who wish to develop their practice. In the Preface, I explained that I would use the analogy of the *Highway Code* to offer guidance and advice on various elements of your teaching journey. As far as possible, this book has been evidence-based, drawing on my primary and secondary research data as well as on my own experiences in the classroom. It was my intention to keep the theoretical side to a minimum and to provide you with practical advice and guidance on how to cope with a range of typical professional scenarios. I hope you feel that I have realized these intentions.

You will no doubt also have noted that a strong theme of 'reflective practice' runs throughout this book; the premise behind this approach is that if teachers do not learn from their mistakes, they will simply continue to make them. It is important to stress that the ideas and strategies offered within this publication are not to be seen as prescriptive. Although these strategies have worked well for me over the years, it is up to you to adapt and temper them to suit your own personality, teaching style and the needs of your pupils. I am confident that I have furnished you with a number of potentially workable strategies that will help to improve the quality of the teaching and learning in your lessons. What I also hope I have done is to encourage you to adopt a proactive approach towards your practice, by getting you to ask pertinent questions about your teaching and about your pupils' learning. If, having read this book, you feel more able to identify and respond positively to the numerous 'watershed' moments that occur in your everyday professional life, my efforts will have been rewarded.

So, where could you go from here? If you liked the idea of using a semiotic approach to support your understanding of the teaching and learning process, you might like to adopt a similar approach when teaching your own pupils. There is a great deal of mileage in using signs from the *Highway Code,* from health and safety manuals and from other sources to make your teaching and learning points; you just need to be creative about doing this. You could, for example, use signs and symbols in your Key Stage 2, 3, 4 and 5 lessons to summarize key points in revision lessons and to highlight the 'dos' and 'don'ts' of examination/ testing protocol. You could use a semiotic approach in a primary school context to launch your rules about how your pupils should behave in 'circle time'. Using signs in this way can really help to cater for pupils who are visual learners, and provide them with additional opportunities to develop their deep learning. If you do not feel that you have the level of creativity required to use the skill of 'bisociation' (ie relating one idea to another), then seek advice from those who do. There is no rule that says you only have to use your own ideas in your lessons. Teaching is a collegiate profession and the sharing and exchanging of ideas, skills and knowledge is to be highly encouraged.

Alternatively, you could create a series of signs and symbols to portray various aspects of the hidden curriculum in your classroom. Many of the signs used in this book to help beginning teachers establish and maintain positive learning scenarios could be used to similar purpose with pupils in a classroom. For example, it would be relatively easy to adapt many of the *Highway Code* signs and relate them to your expectations of pupils' learning and social behaviours. You could even get the pupils to discuss these expectations and then to produce these signs for display in your classroom.

If you are reading this as a professional tutor, mentor or initial teacher trainer, you might like to consider adopting a semiotic approach when training your colleagues. Experience has shown me that most of us respond in some way to the signs and symbols that surround us in our everyday lives. Using these signs as metaphors and analogies for the professional scenarios of my beginning teachers has proved to be a highly effective way of developing their pedagogical learning. I have found that these teachers respond extremely well when being asked to use these visual images to explore the 'dos' and 'don'ts' of their professional practice and there is no doubt that this approach is successful in creating a high level of debate and discussion in training sessions.

Finally, I want to return to my initial premise of teaching being a journey. Just as you only really learn to drive once you have passed your test, so too do you only really learn to teach when the confines of your assessment have been eliminated and when, as an NQT, you lose your 'L plates'. I can assure you that your journey will not be seamless. There are bound to be obstacles in the way, traffic jams, diversions and accidents en route, but hopefully the approach adopted in this book will help you to negotiate these hazards with skill and to plan future journeys in a more reflective and proactive manner. I wish you every success.

Bibliography

Text references

Bell, J. and Dixie, G. (2009) *The Trainee Primary Teacher's Handbook.* London: Continuum.

Bentham, S. (2005) *A Teaching Assistant's Guide to Managing Behaviour in the Classroom.* London: Routledge.

Butt, G. (2006) *Lesson Planning.* Continuum: London.

Dalton, J. and Smith, D. (1986) *Extending Children's Special Abilities.* Victoria: Ministry of Education.

DfE (2010) *The Importance of Teaching.* London: Her Majesty's Stationery Office.

Dixie, G. (2005) *Getting on with Kids in Secondary Schools.* Dereham: Peter Francis Publishers.

Dixie, G. (2007) *Managing Your Classroom.* London: Continuum.

Dixie, G. (2009a) *The Trainee Secondary Teacher's Handbook.* London: Continuum.

Dixie, G. and Bell, J. (2009b) *The Trainee Secondary Teacher's Handbook.* London: Continuum.

Dixie, G. (2010) Introducing Creativity to your Teaching. Lecture delivered to Norfolk and Suffolk GTP and SNITT trainees.

Elton Report (1989) *Discipline in Schools.* London: Her Majesty's Stationery Office.

Furlong, J. and Maynard, T. (1995) *Mentoring Student Teachers.* London: Routledge.

HMSO (2006) *Working Together to Safeguard Children.* London: Her Majesty's Stationery Office.

Kaplan, L. J. (1984) *Adolescence: The farewell to childhood.* New York: Simon and Shuster.

Keddie, N. (1976) *Tinker, Taylor … the Myth of Cultural Deprivation.* Harmondsworth: Penguin.

Kyriacou, C. (1986) *Effective Teaching in Schools.* Oxford: Basil Blackwell.

Kyriacou, C. (2007) *Essential Teaching Skills.* Cheltenham: Nelson Thornes.

Rist, R. (1970) 'Student social class and teacher expectations: the self-fulfilling prophecy in ghetto educations', *Harvard Educational Review*, 40

Rogers, B. (1998) *You Know the Fair Rule.* London: Pitman.

Schön, D. (1983) *The Reflective Practitioner.* London: Temple Smith.

Schön, D. (1987) *Educating the Reflective Practitioner.* San Francisco, CA: Jossey-Bass.

Schön, D. (1991) *The Reflective Turn.* New York: Teachers College Press.

Suffolk County Council (2009) *Introduction to Safeguarding.* Delegate workbook, August.

Willis, P. (1979) *Learning to Labour.* Farnborough: Saxon House.

Wragg, E. C. and Brown, G. (2001) *Questioning in the Primary School.* London: RoutledgeFalmer.

Wragg, T. (1984) *Classroom Teaching Skills: Research findings of the teacher education project.* London: Croom Helm.

Wragg, T. (1995) Teachers' first encounters with their classes, in B. Moon and A. Shelton, *Teaching and Learning in Secondary School.* London: Open University.

Website references

Centre of Studies in Inclusive Education (http://inclusion.uwe.ac.uk/csie/csiefaqs.htm)

Every Child Matters http://publications.everychildmatters.gov.uk/eOrdering-Download/CM5860.pdf

Fischer Family Trust http://www.fischertrust.org/

Maslow http://changingminds.org/explanations/needs/maslow.htm

SEN Code of Practice www.teachernet.gov.uk/docbank/index.cfm?id=3724

Working Together to Safeguard Children: A guide to inter-agency working to safeguard and promote the welfare of children http://publications.dcsf.gov.uk/default.aspx?PageFunction=productdetails&PageMode=publications&ProductId=DCSF-00305-2010&

Index

Lightning Source UK Ltd.
Milton Keynes UK
UKOW05f0750050815

256412UK00007B/180/P